A Vejigante walks in front of a jeep
with a Vejigante mask as a hood ornament

St. James in the Streets

The Religious Processions of Loíza Aldea, Puerto Rico

by

Edward C. Zaragoza

Drew Studies in Liturgy, No. 2

The Scarecrow Press, Inc.
Lanham, Md., and London

SCARECROW PRESS, INC.

Published in the United States of America
by Scarecrow Press, Inc.
4720 Boston Way
Lanham, Maryland 20706

4 Pleydell Gardens, Folkestone
Kent CT20 2DN, England

British Cataloguing-in-Publication Information Available

Library of Congress Cataloging-in-Publication Data

Zaragoza, Edward C.
St. James in the streets : the religious processions of Loíza Aldea, Puerto
Rico / by Edward C. Zaragoza.
p.   cm. — (Drew studies in liturgy ; no. 2)
Includes bibliographical references and index.
1. St. James' Day—Puerto Rico—Loíza Aldea. 2. Festivals—Puerto
Rico—Loíza Aldea. 3. Processions—Puerto Rico— Loíza Aldea.
4. James, the Greater, Saint—Cults. 5. Taíno Indians—Religion. 6. Taíno
Indians—Rites and ceremonies. 7. Loíza Aldea (P.R.)—Religious life and
customs. 8. Loíza Aldea (P.R.)—Social life and customs. 9. Loíza Aldea
(P.R.) I. Title. II. Series.
GT4995J.35Z37   1995   394.2'66—dc   CIP

ISBN 0-8108-3070-1 (cloth : alk. paper)

⊖™ The paper used in this publication meets the minimum requirements of
American National Standard for Information Sciences—Permanence of
Paper for Printed Library Materials, ANSI Z39.48–1984.
Manufactured in the United States of America.

In Memory of
Miss Carmen Zaragoza
(1918-1993)

CONTENTS

EDITORS' FOREWORD

One of the fruits of the liturgical renewal movement in the late twentieth century has been renewed attention to study of the liturgy in all of the churches. This monograph series aims to publish some of the best of this new scholarship. Fresh studies of Episcopal, Roman Catholic, and Orthodox liturgy will be included, along with studies of the full range of Protestant liturgies.

Much liturgical writing to date has concentrated on liturgy as text. This series will not ignore such studies, but seeks to reflect more recent thinking that understands liturgy not only against the background of theological principle, liturgical tradition and ritual text, but also in terms of liturgical practice and setting.

Clarity of focus, relative brevity, and freshness of scholarly contribution will be the principal criteria for publication. Revised dissertations will be considered. Edited collections of essays and texts may be included when they have a unified topical focus which may significantly advance scholarship in the field.

As the second number in the series we are pleased to publish a monograph about the religious processions of a former slave community in Puerto Rico, which honor St. James the Apostle annually. This study was produced by one of the graduates of Drew University's Graduate Program in Liturgy, Ted Zaragoza of Phillips Theological Seminary.

Robin A. Leaver, Westminster Choir College of Rider University and Drew University

Kenneth E. Rowe, Drew University

PREFACE

Festivals are moments of conviviality; they are times when people come together to celebrate. Time set apart, fiestas are boisterous, colorful, full of life. Sometimes even to participants, they can be daunting physically or emotionally. To an outsider, the vast array of sights, sounds, smells, and sheer humanity can be overwhelming. To understand what is happening, the visitor needs a sympathetic guide who can "unpack" the symbol systems which undergird the merrymaking.

In this monograph, Edward Zaragoza is just such a guide. He helps us to comprehend the complexities of the fiesta of St. James the Apostle in Loíza Aldea, Puerto Rico. As our guide he grounds the sociopolitical situation of modern Puerto Rico. With both the keen eye of a liturgist and an ethnographer, he paints a verbal picture of the fiesta. And so we are able to join in with him and the pilgrims as they traverse the town, both symbolically and literally.

He reminds us that fiestas operate on several levels-- the "now" of the pilgrims blend with years past, each in turn shaping what future fiestas will be like. By analyzing two central symbols of the fiesta--the three statues of St. James and the four masked figures which accompany the statues on the pilgrimage--we come to understand the worldview of the worshippers.

Using Victor Turner, Arnold van Gennep, Roger Bastide, and Roberto DaMatta to ground his analysis, he explores the status and power hierarchies of Loíza Aldea and how they can be "read" in the ritual masks and the statues. In detailed discussions the reader discovers the sex/gender system of the town, its present day complex ethnic and racial relationships, its economic tribulations. He documents continuing African religious influences on

ix

the fiesta's masked characters and intriguingly, points out possible signs of the Taíno faith's influence as well.

In an anthropological *tour de force*, Edward Zaragoza allows his readers to join with the pilgrims "who walk the fesitval route ...who perform the age old story of the beginnings by their participation in the fiesta, [as we] walk among African and Taíno images as well as the Christian saint and devil" (pp. 156-157). We learn how iconography and behavior, faith and life simultaneously construct each other. This book takes us on a journey of a people and their faith; a journey which reaches into the past yet is made visible in the present day fiestas. It is a journey with an uncertain future. It is the story of their faith in themselves and in their God, a story well told.

Kathleen S. Lowney, Valdosta State University

1

PORTRAITS OF ST. JAMES THE APOSTLE

INTRODUCTION

Fifteen miles east of San Juan, Puerto Rico, there is a former slave community that dates its beginnings from the earliest years of the Spanish conquest of the New World. Once the site of an Taíno Arawak Indian village, and later a small but important producer of sugarcane, this community continues a religious tradition brought to the New World by the Spaniards. In a style that is distinctly its own, Loíza Aldea each year celebrates its patron saint, St. James the Apostle, with a fiesta. This study is an analysis of that fiesta.

According to Iberian tradition, St. James the Apostle is portrayed in his historic role as defender and protector of Spain. Originally a pilgrim who traveled to Spain preaching the Gospel, St. James the Apostle became a heavenly soldier on horseback, sword unsheathed, the slayer of Spain's greatest enemy in the Middle Ages, the Moors. In Loíza Aldea, this tradition is repeated but with a twist. Here the saint is portrayed not only as the divine military hero of a time long ago, but also as the friend of all Loiceños. As a way of underscoring this friendship, each major segment of the town, that is, the men, the women, and the children, has a separate likeness of St. James the Apostle to whom they can appeal for aid.

1

In the fiesta, in addition to parading the statues representing the saint, four masked figures reenact his exploits. The reenactment of the saint's deeds by masked figures, as well as his representation in the form of a statue, are common throughout Latin America. But again, like the statues of Loíza Aldea, these masked figures are localized versions of a larger tradition. Although these masked figures include the customary saint and Moor characters that are essential to the legend of the saint, we will see that each is costumed according to Loíza Aldea's own traditions. We will also meet two other characters who appear to be indigenous constructions, the old man and the crazy woman.

In the statues of St. James the Apostle and in the masked figures, we have two different but overlapping portrayals of the saint. It is the relationship between these two portrayals that is the focus of this study. Neither portrayal alone presents the full meaning which the saint has for Loíza Aldea. And although each presentation originates in a larger Iberian context, it is in the manner in which Loíza Aldea transforms each presentation of the saint into its own image that we see their particular portraits of the saint. These portraits depict St. James the Apostle as one who turns social structures upside down much as he did when he turned the Moorish occupation of Spain on its head in the Middle Ages.

A dual emphasis on the statues, on the one hand, and on the masked figures, on the other, leads to inevitable problems regarding how each set is to be interpreted. The work of Brazilian anthropologist Roberto DaMatta is very helpful for interpreting the symbolism involved in carrying statues of St. James the Apostle in the fiesta's religious processions. The carrying of statues signals a process whereby the boundaries of two ordinarily separate social domains, namely that of the men (the street) and that of the women (the home), interpenetrate. This is possible because the presence of the saint creates a new domain wherein this interpenetration is possible.

This interpretation is credible when we recognize with DaMatta that the heart of the symbolization process is the movement of a person or object from one domain to another.[1] This movement he calls dislocation. Through the process of dislocation, persons and objects can be exaggerated, reinforced, inverted, dissimulated, neutralized, diminished, or omitted.[2] The result of a movement between domains is that a symbol emerges that becomes the central metaphor of the ritual at hand and which links the domains that have been involved in the dislocation process.[3] From this process, the meaning of the ritual is revealed, and that meaning is something fundamental to the culture.

The key to the interpretation of the masked figures is found in the fact that they are just that, masked figures. Masking does not serve a single purpose. In the case of the masked figures of Loíza Aldea, the category which I will argue makes the most sense out of their masks and costumes is that of the clown or fool. A well-known character in European literature, the fool or clown as trickster also has a home in African mythology. Fools customarily "uncrown"[4] a person of high authority such as a king, bishop, or saint, and bring him down to earth. In so doing, fools open a door not only to how ordinary people see their saints, but also to how they see themselves. Saints and people change places with one another.

We will see that the traditions surrounding the figure of the fool are rich in associations. In the fiesta for St. James the Apostle in Loíza Aldea, fools take on the dimension of archetypes. As archetypes, the fools of the fiesta draw on the the fools found in local history. In each of Loíza Aldea's historical and cultural influences, the Spanish, African, and Taíno Arawak, we can discern parallels when we discuss the masked figures in detail. We will see that each cultural example of the archetype displays the customary purpose of the fool as acting out status reversals or displacing that which was thought to be fixed in its place. In this fiesta for St. James the Apostle, saints become clowns, and clowns becomes saints.

THESIS

My analysis of the fiesta for St. James the Apostle in Loíza Aldea is limited in scope. It intentionally concentrates on the fiesta's three days of religious processions because these religious processions are the primary context for the appearance of both the statues of the saint and the masked figures. The basic premise governing the analysis is that the fiesta tells us something about Loíza Aldea. The fiesta is the village's reflection about its life. On the one hand, the fiesta tells us how the village believes life should be, and, on the other hand, how the village knows life to be. Both views are brought out into the open for all to see. St. James the Apostle, represented as a warrior in his statues, displays how village life should be: faithful, uncompromising, victorious. The masked figures, as fools, dare to show how village life really is: ambiguous, ironic, contradictory. The fiesta for St. James the Apostle, then, is the village holding a mirror up to itself in its portraits of the saint. In the fiesta, the village of Loíza Aldea reveals itself to itself.[5]

This self-revelation takes place in the interaction between the saint and the masked figures. The saint represents the ideal, the masked figures the real. But it is only in their sharing of the same space in the religious processions that the self-reflection of Loíza Aldea is fully displayed. In the religious processions the sacred and the mundane reverse status. St. James the Apostle comes down to the level of the people, and the people are raised to the level of the saint. This transference occurs both in the new domain created by the appearance of the statues of the saint and in the antics of the masked figures. In both instances, boundaries are crossed, and in the crossing, a new domain is created. This domain is the simultaneous presence of how life should be and how life really is. This is the creation of a new domain that creates a new reality, however temporary: the ideal within the real.

THE STRUCTURE

Following this introductory chapter, the second chapter presents a historical narrative about Puerto Rico. This chapter, "From Conquest to Colonization," places the fiesta for St. James the Apostle in the larger context of Puerto Rican history. This is important because the history of Loíza Aldea is in many ways a microcosm of the island's history. The town has felt the full impact of all of the vicissitudes of the island's history, as we will see.

The third chapter, "The Fiesta of Santiago Apóstol," centers on the fiesta as it is today, paying particular attention to the three days of religious processions in which the statues of the saint make their appearance. Included in this chapter is a discussion of the roots and traditions which are the foundations of the fiesta. The masked figures, who also make their appearance during the three days of religious processions, are the focus of the fourth chapter. In this chapter, "The Ritual Clowns," the masked figures are interpreted as ritual clowns, that is, as boundary figures who turn social conventions upside down, as evidenced by their behavior. As we will see, the fools of European literature and the tricksters of African mythology share a common penchant for disrupting the status quo for their own amusement and for the injection of novel possibilities into social relationships.

My interpretation of the masked figures parallels Don Handelman's discussion of ritual clowns. For Handleman, ritual clowns, as agents of anti-structure,[6] are opposed to deity-figures.[7] Their oppositional stance creates a commentary upon the status quo.[8] This commentary is possible, states Handelman, because ritual clowns are ambiguous. They straddle the worlds that exist on each side of the boundary. Handelman is also a refreshing change from much of the literature on ritual clowns. He refuses to bow to psychological explanations regarding what ritual clowns do, preferring to concentrate on how they work as liminal characters.

In the fifth chapter, "The Taínos and the Fiesta," I locate in Taíno Arawak Indian creator gods a fertile field that complements the double nature found in Spanish and African tricksters. Though an Indian influence on the fiesta cannot be proven, this chapter suggests that the archetype of the trickster found in each of the three cultures makes an Indian influence plausible.

These chapters are successive and yet they stand on top of each other. They are meant to be read in sequence while being bundled together at the same time. With each chapter we can see more deeply into possible meanings and roots of the fiesta. This study begins with history and ends with anthropology. It begins with sequential events and ends with homologies. It begins with paraded metonyms and ends with suggestive metaphors.

ABOUT SOURCES

To my knowledge there has been only one book written about the fiesta of St. James the Apostle in Loíza Aldea. That book, *La Fiesta de Santiago Apóstol en Loíza Aldea* (The Fiesta of St. James the Apostle in Loíza Aldea), was written by Puerto Rican anthropologist Ricardo E. Alegría, originally as a master's thesis, in 1954. *La Fiesta de Santiago Apóstol en Loíza Aldea* is a monograph which describes the fiesta, its history, and organization. Included in the work are also excellent descriptions of the masked figures and their traditional roles. Other than my own fieldwork, it has been my primary source of information regarding the fiesta.

Another important source of information has been an unpublished M.A. thesis written by Father David L. Ungerlieder Kepler. His work, *Fiestas Afro-Borincanas y Cambio Social en Puerto Rico: El Caso de Loíza* (Afro-Boricuan Fiestas and Social Change in Puerto Rico: The Case of Loíza), written in 1983, borrows heavily from Alegría's work on the fiesta. Its main contribution to my work is its discussion of the economic and social history of the village.

The only other source I have found which deals with the fiesta is a videotape produced by Producciones Vejigantes, Inc. and La Fundación de las Humanidades Puertorriqueñas (Vejigante Productions, Inc. and The Foundation for Puerto Rican Humanities). The videotape, "Las Fiestas de Santiago Apóstol en Loíza" (The Fiestas of St. James the Apostle in Loíza), records the fiesta of 1982. It also includes brief interviews with Puerto Rican scholars about the history of the fiesta, the masks and disguises worn, and the African contributions to Loíza Aldea's music and dancing.

THEORIES AND METHODS

The fiesta of St. James the Apostle in Loíza Aldea is a complex cultural event. Because of its complexities, I have sought out theories and methods which promised assistance in gaining access to the fiesta and its system of symbols. Since the fiesta is a complex mesh of relationships, no one theory or method, no one way of looking at the material can plumb the depths of the fiesta. Following the "toolbox approach" of historian of religions Wendy Doniger O'Flaherty, I have adopted and adapted a complex of theories and methods to investigate the raw material of the fiesta of St. James the Apsotle in Loíza Aldea.

O'Flaherty offers this rationale for using "the toolbox approach":

> When one is confronting a body of raw material (and this is the first step in any original analysis), it is good to have tucked away somewhere in one's mind all the patterns that other scholars have seen in other materials, all the ways in which they have tried to solve analogous problems. In this way one develops a vocabulary in which to recognize and express the patterns that appear in the new corpus and to formulate new patterns as the need arises. The material itself will usually suggest what is the most appropriate pattern to look for at each point.[9]

Since I am investigating a cultural phenomenon, I begin by looking to anthropologist Clifford Geertz to provide me with a basic understanding of how to look at that phenomenon.

Clifford Geertz

The writings of Clifford Geertz have provided me with a basic anatomy of interpretive anthropological theory which has enabled me to research and write about the fiesta. Three major ideas of his have made particularly important contributions to my thinking about the fiesta. These ideas are that 1) ethnography is interpretation,[10] 2) a culture is an ensemble of texts that can be read by the anthropologist,[11] and 3) religious symbols are meaningful because they fuse a culture's worldview and ethos.[12]

Anthropology interprets culture as it describes it. The interpretation, even at its best, is incomplete and contestable.[13] This is because cultural analysis is a process of guessing at the meanings of the culture, assessing those guesses, and then, from the best of them, drawing plausible conclusions.[14] This is why Geertz can describe anthropological writings as "fictive." They are "made up" in that they are constructed out of the imagination of the anthropologist as he or she encounters the culture.[15] This does not mean that the interpretation is false. It means that the interpretation is open to challenge and revision. Increasing intelligibility within the complexity of the culture is the goal of anthropology, not the construction of eternal laws.

As an ensemble of texts, a culture has a story to tell that can be read by the anthropologist. For Geertz, cultures contain within themselves the interpretation.[16] The problem for the anthropologist is gaining access to the hidden interpretation. One entrance is through the system of religious symbols.

There are three crucial ingredients to Geertz's understanding of religion as a cultural system: worldview, ethos, and symbol. A worldview is a culture's metaphysics, its comprehensive view of reality. An ethos is a culture's style of life and its ethics. Each reflects and reinforces the other in that together they grant ultimacy to the worldview with its view of how the world is ordered, and authority to the ethos with its social norms and values.[17] The result is that life has meaning. The tangible formulation of this fusion of worldview and ethos is the religious symbol.[18] When a religious symbol, or a cluster of religious symbols, is publically displayed in ritual, the fund of general meanings about the world and the individual's place in it, which are stored in the symbols, is opened to the participants.[19] This opening up of meaning takes place in ritual because a ritual is the enactment of the worldview which gives rise to the religious conviction of the ethos.[20]

Victor W. Turner

Adding to my fund of knowledge regarding symbols and how they work are the ideas of Victor W. Turner. For Turner, symbols have three basic properties, namely, multivocality, unity, and polarization. Symbols are multivocal because they have a wide spectrum of referents. They are unified in that they relate disparate associations. And symbols are polarized because in them can be found both the ideological and orectic poles. The ideological pole corresponds to the norms and values in the social order. The orectic pole corresponds to the desires and feelings aroused in the person by sensory stimuli.[21]

Along with describing the properties inherent in symbols, Turner divides symbols into dominant and instrumental categories according to their place in ritual. Dominant symbols represent the center, or the end, of the ritual. They are constant and fixed. Instrumental symbols are what their name implies. They lead the participant in the ritual to the dominant symbol. Since they do not represent the end of the ritual, instrumental symbols depend on the relationships among all the symbols in the ritual for their meaning.[22]

Claude Lévi-Strauss

As summarized above, the work of Geertz and Turner have provided me with theories which have formed the foundation of this study. Their insights into the nature of ritual and symbol have been signposts which in many ways have determined the direction of this work. But it is to Claude Lévi-Strauss that I owe my initial insights into the fiesta for St. James the Apostle.

Lévi-Strauss gave me my first hints as to how the statues of the saint related to one another, how they related to the masked figures, and how the masked figures related to themselves. In his massive study of myths, Lévi-Strauss postulated that myth is a response to a contradiction in life. Myths work by breaking up reality into thinkable blocks. These blocks are of high generality and take the shape of binary oppositions in need of mediation. As the initial block of oppositions is mediated, it generates a transformation of itself in the form of another dichotomy in need of mediation. This process may be virtually endless. Through the permutations or transformations generated by the initial dichotomy, contradiction strives for resolution in the form of mediation. If a resolution is reached through this process (and this does not occur if the contradiction is real), meaning emerges in the form of a paradigm. This paradigm can then be applied to the contradiction at hand. Using this model of Lévi-Strauss's, each of the three sets of relationships in the fiesta are basically oppositional and in need of mediation. We will see in chapter three that one of the statues of the saint mediates between the other two. Chapter four discusses the drive for mediation between two contradictory views of life represented, on the one hand, by the statues of the saint, and, on the other hand, by the masked figures. In chapter five the masked figures break into two sets of binary oppositions. They relate to each other as pairs of oppositions, and they relate to each other within pairs of oppositions. They also relate to each other as transformations of each other. It is this model that has guided how I have configured, in their most general terms, the symbolic relationships within the fiesta.

FIELDWORK AND INFORMANTS

I traveled to Puerto Rico at least once a year from 1985-1988 and again in 1991. Each time I stayed there for up to two weeks at a time. I attended the fiesta of St. James the Apostle in Loíza Aldea during the month of July in 1986, 1988 and 1991. The other excursions have been to interview scholars, to meet with Puerto Rican social agencies as part of Professor David Graybeal's annual winter trip to Puerto Rico for the seminarians of the Drew Theological School, and to "soak up" the culture through its beaches, mountains, food, dance, and people.

In January 1987 I interviewed Ricardo E. Alegría, Puerto Rico's foremost anthropologist and driving force behind the government's efforts at preserving many of the landmarks in Old San Juan. I took this opportunity to ask

Alegría about the possibility of an Indian influence on the fiesta. Chapter five will argue against Alegría's contention that there is no Indian influence on the fiesta. I also had the opportunity to discuss my work with Miguel Rodríguez López, a Puerto Rican archeologist, who confirmed my intuition regarding an Indian contribution to the fiesta. He encouraged me to pursue it.

In Loíza Aldea, I am indebted to the hospitality of Pastora Carrasquillo, wife of Don Castor Ayala, and her family, who carry on the tradition of making *vejigante* masks for the fiesta. Whenever I traveled to Puerto Rico, I made a point of stopping at the Ayala Art Shop, hoping to have a chance to speak with her. Often in the company of her daughter, Carrasquillo answered my questions regarding the fiesta without hesitation, often adding her own criticisms of a particular fiesta. It is from her that I first heard the legend of Santiago Apóstol.

Pedro LaViera, another mask maker in Loíza Aldea, graciously shared with me how *vejigante* masks were made one morning. He allowed me to photograph the process and answered all of my queries, especially about the possibility of a political side to the fiesta.

Samuel Lind, another artist in Loíza Aldea, chronicles the changes in the fiesta, and highlights one aspect of it each year through his serigraphs. Lind has been generous in showing me around his work shop. He has also helped me see how the fiesta changes a little each year, especially with regard to the preponderance of one masked figure over another.

Educators at Interamerican University who have become friends over the past several years, Professor Carmen Collazo and her husband, the former Chancellor at Interamerican University, Gamaliel Pérez Santiago, have made sure that I experienced everyday Puerto Rico and not only the "tourist traps" of Ashford Avenue's hotels in Condado.[23] I am also grateful for the hospitality of their home and family.[24]

In March 1988, I presented an earlier draft of the chapter on the ritual clowns at the annual meeting of *Encuentro Caribeño* (A Caribbean Meeting) at the San Germán campus of Interamerican University. The paper was received favorably by Puerto Rican scholars from around the world, and their few corrective comments provided me with some very important feedback. The paper, "The Santiago Apóstol of Loíza, Puerto Rico," was published in 1990 in *Caribbean Studies*, the journal of The Institute for Caribbean Studies at the University of Puerto Rico.

CONTRIBUTIONS TO FIELDS OF STUDY

Liturgical Studies

In the field of liturgical studies there has long been an overemphasis on the study of written texts. In this analysis of the fiesta of St. James the Apostle in Loíza Aldea the people are the primary text. This study, like its subject, is in part about a "liturgy of the streets," a public work of the people. As a liturgy, a Christian form of ritual performance, the meanings of the fiesta's symbols cannot be abstracted from their human context. Opening up the field of liturgy is important. The fiesta as liturgy is more than a mnemonic device recalling the village's local history, ethnic identity, social relationships, and religious convictions.[25] The fiesta as liturgy allows for the reality of a noneucharistic *anamnesis*,[26] the simultaneous commemoration of St. James the Apostle and the making present of him in the lives of the Loiceños. This *anamnesis* connects the Loiceños to their history, identity, society, and religion in a way that includes their Afro-Boricuan spirits as well as their Christian saint.

Caribbean Studies

As noted above, the fiesta of St. James the Apostle in Loíza Aldea has received limited treatment even from Puerto Rican scholars although its existence is widely known and alluded to in many books that discuss Puerto Rico's distinctive cultural expressions. This study adds to the field of Puerto Rican cultural studies because it explores and illuminates the symbols in one of the island's oldest and most authentic festivals. My work will also contribute to the several fields of Caribbean Studies because the fiesta is an expression of both the unity and diversity found in the cultural expressions of the region that emerged out of slavery.

Masks and Masking

In the field of masks, masking, and masquerade, this study offers no new theory for symbolic anthropologists, but it does offer another splendid example of how masks and costumes are loaded with symbolic meaning when incorporated into a ritual like a religious procession. The discussion of the relationships among the masqueraders in the fiesta is a major part of this study.

CONCLUSION

In order to write this work I have had to wear several masks. I have been a detective searching for clues, a cryptologist deciphering codes, an historian tracing the sequence of events, a participant-observer racing around like a news reporter trying to record what I was seeing, and an amateur photographer worried that my photographs would be out of focus. Much was learned by trial and error; much was accomplished with a good bit of luck.

It is important to add that although Puerto Ricans residing on the mainland will tell you that "everything in Puerto Rico is political," this is not a study about Puerto Rican politics or about "the status question."[27] To attempt to write such a work would indeed take the analysis of the fiesta of Santiago Apóstol in an entirely different direction, a direction already followed by Fr. Ungerlieder Kepler.

Nor is this study about the changes that take place in the individual who dons a mask, unless, as stated above, I am writing about myself. Like the masked figures in the fiesta, I have revealed a bit of myself to the discerning reader in the writing of this study. I will have succeeded in making the fiesta intelligible if the reader finds a part of himself or herself reflected in it.

I have not tried to answer ultimate questions. That is not the place of anthropology. I have tried to offer an interpretation of the fiesta that, for me, emerges out of the fiesta. If the reader has found his or her way to seeing these perspectives, I am satisfied with my efforts.

NOTES

1. Roberto DaMatta, "Carnival in Multiple Planes," in *Rite, Drama, Festival, Spectacle: Rehearsals Toward a Theory of Cultural Performance*, ed. John J. MacAloon (Philadelphia: Institute for the Study of Human Issues, Inc., 1984), 214.

2. *Ibid.*, 215.

3. *Ibid.*, 216.

4. I have borrowed this term from Mikhail Bakhtin. See his book *Rabelais and His World*, trans. Helene Iswolsky (Cambridge, Massachusetts: The M.I.T. Press, 1968), 214.

5. Robert Anthony Orsi, *The Madonna of 115th Street: Faith and Community in Italian Harlem, 1880-1950* (New Haven: Yale University Press, 1985), xxii.

6. *Anti-structure* is Victor W. Turner's term for that which stands over against the status quo.

7. Don Handelman, "The Ritual Clown: Attributes and Affinities," *Anthropos* 76 (1981): 322.

8. *Ibid.*, 325.

9. Wendy Doniger O'Flaherty, *Women, Androgynes, and Other Mythical Beasts* (Chicago: The University of Chicago Press, 1980), 5.

10. Clifford Geertz, "Thick Description: Toward an Interpretive Theory of Culture," in *The Interpretation of Cultures: Selected Essays* (New York: Basic Books, 1973), 15.

11. Clifford Geertz, "Deep Play: Notes on the Balinese Cockfight," in *The Interpretation of Cultures: Selected Essays* (New York: Basic Books, 1973), 452.

12. Clifford Geertz, "Religion As a Cultural System," in *The Interpretation of Cultures: Selected Essays* (New York: Basic Books, 1973), 90.

13. Geertz, "Thick Description," 29.

14. *Ibid.*, 20.

15. *Ibid.*, 15.

16. Geertz, "Deep Play," 453.

17. Geertz, "Religion As a Cultural System," 112.

18. *Ibid.*, 91, 113.

19. Clifford Geertz, "Ethos, World View, and the Analysis of Sacred Symbols," in *The Interpretation of Cultures: Selected Essays* (New York: Basic Books, 1973), 127.

20. Geertz, "Religion As a Cultural System," 113-114.

21. Victor W. Turner and Edith Turner, *Image and Pilgrimage in Christian Culture* (New York: Columbia University Press, 1978), 246-247.

22. *Ibid.*, 245-246.

23. To balance the fine cuisine of "La Reina de España" (The Queen of Spain) restaurant in Condado, they ensured the scope of my experience by inviting me to sample the traditional food of Puerto Rico's working class at "El Obrero" (The Worker) in Río Piedras.

24. When I stayed with the Pérez family, I had the opportunity to hear many stories which showed me how passionate Puerto Ricans are about their *patria* (motherland) as well as jokes which led me into another level of Puerto Rico's cultural distinctiveness.

25. Joseph Sciorra, "Religious Processions in Italian Williamsburg," *Drama Review* 29 (Fall 1985): 65.

26. *Anamnesis* is a technical liturgical term. It usually signifies the part of the eucharistic prayer (anaphora) which explicitly states that the church is offering the bread and the cup in remembrance of Christ. My use of the term is generic. Anamnesis is an action whereby the person or event commemorated is actually made present. See *The New Westminster Dictionary of Liturgy and Worship*, ed. by J.G. Davies (Philadelphia: The Westminster Press, 1986), 18.

27. "The status question" is the name given to Puerto Rico's ambiguous political status vis-à-vis the United States. At present the island is neither an independent country nor the 51st state. The island is "a free associated state," that is, a possession or territory of the United States. This relationship was formalized in 1952.

2

FROM CONQUEST TO COLONIZATION

INTRODUCTION

The purpose of this chapter is to locate the fiesta of St. James the Apostle in Loíza Aldea, Puerto Rico, in a larger historical context. This contextualization is important because the only date given for the beginning of the fiesta is 1832.[1] This date is an interesting bit of data because by 1832 Puerto Rico was changing from an economy based upon small-scale subsistence farming to an economy based, in large part, on a *hacienda* (plantation) system of sugar production.[2] Producing sugar for export was expensive, requiring large numbers of workers. Slavery, an inexpensive source of labor, provided the workers necessary for sugar production on the island to be profitable. In the nineteenth century, Loíza Aldea became one of the fourteen sugar-producing areas in Puerto Rico.[3]

The story behind the parallel development of the sugar economy and slavery in Puerto Rico is a long and complicated one. While it is not within the purview of this study to discuss this story in great detail, a grasp of the outline of the story is important for situating the discussions of the fiesta which appear in following chapters. The leading figures in this story are not the plantation owners nor the slaves. They are, rather, two great institutions: the Spanish Crown and the Roman Catholic Church. The expansion of the sugar economy and the growth of slavery in Puerto Rico were rooted in the formidable partnership between these two great powers.

Their partnership fused the profit motive of the Crown with the religious prejudice of the Church.[4] The Crown needed an inexpensive, disciplined work force to insure profits from its colony. The Church encouraged the Crown's policies and practices of slavery in part because of its disdain for the religious beliefs and rituals of the slaves who were, in the view of the Church, "infidels" in need of salvation. The enslavement of the indigenous Taíno Arawak Indian population and the blacks from West Africa in Puerto Rico provided the Church with a captive audience for its proselytizing.[5] While the Crown controlled an individual's person, the Church attempted to control the individual's soul.

This partnership between the Crown and the Church was not one contrived for Spain's exploits in the New World. It had a long history. In the thirteenth-century code, *Las Siete Partidas* (the Seven Laws of Castile compiled by King Alfonso X), slavery was recognized as a valid means of promoting Spain's economy. It was based upon the Justinian Code, which, in turn, was a synthesis of Roman and Canon law.[6] *Las Siete Partidas* postulated three categories of individuals, three types of slaves, and the rights allowed slaves. The three categories of individuals were free, slave, and freed. Slaves were enemies of the Roman Catholic Church who were taken as prisoners of war, children of slaves, and those individuals who, for whatever reason, had relinquished their liberty. The rights allowed to slaves were to be honored even against the demands of their owners. These rights included the right to private property, the right to marriage, the right to manumission, that could sometimes be purchased with a slave's private property, and the right to be free from suffering and death at the hands of an owner.[7]

For its part, the Roman Catholic Church considered slavery just and inevitable. It grounded its policy in both scripture and tradition. Since scripture did not condemn slavery, it was allowed. Moreover, St. Paul and St. Thomas postulated that slavery was the result of sin or the moral inferiority of the individual prior to enslavement. Since the Church originally was about the business of saving souls from sin, slavery was considered to be an important and useful tool for the propagation of Christianity. After all, in the eyes of the Church, the fate of one's eternal soul was vastly more important than the loss of one's personal freedom. Slavery, therefore, was for the Church a legitimate means for converting individuals from sinners into saints.[8]

In the fifteenth century, Spain began discriminating against individuals based primarily upon their ethnicity and religious beliefs. A policy of *limpieza de sangre* (blood purity) began with the *Reconquista* (Reconquest) when Spain defeated and enslaved the Moors, and it continued later that same century when Spain expelled the Jews. Parallel to this concept of blood purity was the distinction between "Old Christians" and "New Christians." Old Christians were those who could trace their Spanish-Catholic bloodlines back to the Middle Ages. New Christians were converts from Judaism or Islam.[9] When we discuss the ethnic identity of Loiceños in chapter three, we will see the lingering effects of the Spanish policy of blood purity.

THE ECONOMIC DEVELOPMENT OF THE ISLAND THROUGH THE NINETEENTH CENTURY

In the sixteenth and seventeenth centuries, Puerto Rico was isolated and economically underdeveloped. Its conquest and colonization began as an economic and religious enterprise that sought to conquer the New World for the glory of the Crown and the glory of God. The indigenous Taíno Arawak Indian population was forced, in the early decades of the conquest, to mine the rivers of Puerto Rico for gold. Though in reality enslaved, the Indians were technically free because they worked with the consent of their *cacique* (chief). In return for their labor, the Indians were under the *encomienda* ("protection") of their *encomenderos* (owners).

Many Indians died under this infamous *encomienda* system by falling prey to disease and starvation. Others were killed in the Indian uprisings against the Spaniards. Some committed suicide rather than endure their loss of freedom and the maltreatment of their *encomenderos*. Many of those who survived finally gained their freedom. It is well known that the Roman Catholic Church intervened on behalf of the Indians in an effort to end their suffering at the hands of the colonists. This effort, however, culminated in the large-scale enslavement of blacks from West Africa.

With the depletion of the small deposits of gold on the island, the near decimation of the indigenous Indian population, Puerto Rico became, on the one hand, a military outpost, and on the other hand, an island of subsistence farmers. As a military outpost, Puerto Rico, "the key to the Indies," served as the guardian of Spain's shipping lanes to her colonies in Mexico and Peru where rich deposits of gold had been discovered. The Spaniards, with the help of *ladinos*,[10] took over the subsistence economy of the Indians in cultivating small amounts of corn, potatoes, cassava, tobacco, cotton, pineapples and plantains.[11] Always in need of manufactured goods, the island's inhabitants resorted to smuggling and contraband trade, a practice that continued well into the nineteenth century.

Puerto Rico's economic isolation, and its accompanying agricultural underproduction, was the result of a long-term chronic problem: a dearth of capital and labor. The Spanish Crown had offered land, but not ownership, to Spaniards willing to settle on the island. With the promise of wealth from gold mining gone, the high cost of importing the slaves needed for large-scale farming, frequent attacks by neighboring Caribe Indians, epidemics, and hurricanes, new settlers were discouraged from emigrating to the island.[12]   In fact, many island inhabitants had begun leaving Puerto Rico in order to try their luck at finding gold in South America. This lack of capital and depopulation continued into the seventeenth century.

In addition to this problem, the military stationed in Puerto Rico had to defend the island from more than one attack by the British Navy. Great Britain intended to end Spain's domination of the New World by occupying Puerto Rico. While Great Britain ultimately failed in its attempt, the island's military continued to fortify its defenses using slave labor. The military's efforts were rewarded with the defeat of the Dutch Navy in the seventeenth century. Like the British, the Dutch had their own commerical aspirations that centered on Puerto Rico as a potential foothold in the New World.

Puerto Rico in the seventeenth century was at the mercy of the highly centralized government of Spain, and its military governor on the island, as it had been in the sixteenth. Since the *situados* (subsidies) from the Crown were often insufficient and late in coming, life on the island was slow to change. The military, growing increasingly short of men due to its battles with the British and the Dutch, recruited civilians into military service. A growing free *criollo* (born on the island) population was organized in each *partido* (territorial district) into a *milicia urbana*. These local militias, armed only with sticks, knives, and machetes, were ready to defend their towns, and even the city of San Juan, against attack.[13]

In an effort to expand the colony's economy, cattle were introduced to the island. The colonists ate the meat and sold the hides. Spain's continued resistance to viewing Puerto Rico as anything other than a military outpost in a dependent colony guaranteed further delays in developing the island's sugar industry. The Crown refused to provide the massive injections of capital necessary for purchasing the equipment and slave labor required to operate a profitable sugar industry. What little production there was, was exploited to Spain's advantage and markets.

In the eighteenth century Puerto Rico's economy began to expand, albeit at a much slower pace than her sister colonies of Cuba and Venezuela. One reason for this budding expansion was Spain's war with Great Britain. The British Navy had successfully interrupted Spanish shipping so that Puerto Rico was cut off from her only trading partner. To keep her military outpost in the Caribbean viable, Spain allowed Puerto Rico limited trading with other Caribbean islands, Latin America, and the United States. At this time Puerto Rico began a long history of trading with the United States for staples, like flour, since wheat was unsuccessful as a crop on the island. Puerto Rico also began pirating English ships when they entered nearby waters. However, neither the opening of non-

Spanish ports nor piracy eliminated the need for Puerto
Rico's reliance on contraband trade for badly needed
manufactured goods.

Although an important coffee industry was
beginning in the central highlands, there still was no
significant plantation development at this time on the island
during the eighteenth century.[14] Economic development
remained uneven in the island's predominantly rural society
of small farms and towns. There was, however, a growth
in the population among the free people of color on the
island, who intermingled freely with the whites. This
blurring of social differences through the seventeenth and
early eigtheenth centuries was possible because of the
virtual self-rule of the peasant farmers.[15] Free people of
color worked as domestic servants, seafarers, stevedores,
and peasant farmers.[16] By the end of the century, their
number exceeded the number of slaves on the island. By
1775, there were 35,000 free people of color and 7,000
slaves.[17] This social environment changed drastically with
the emergence of the plantation in the nineteenth century.

With the rapid expansion of the sugar industry in the
nineteenth century, Puerto Rico ended a period which has
been described as three hundred years of stasis.[18] There
were several reasons for this dramatic change in the island's
economy. The Spanish Crown, up until this time, had
assumed the allegiance of its colony of Puerto Rico.
Revolutions in New World colonies such as Venezuela
awakened the Crown to an unsettling reality. The colonists
in Puerto Rico had been clamoring for greater autonomy in
such areas as trade for years. With a revolutionary climate
pervading the region, the Crown was pressed to grant the
colonists in Puerto Rico certain concessions as a way of
insuring their continued loyalty.

These concessions were outlined in the royal decree of 1815, the *Cédula de gracias* (Bill of favor). This decree addressed the central economic concerns of the island: capital, labor, and trade. The Crown reduced or eliminated its high tariffs on imported slaves and on the agricultural machinery crucial for invigorating the island's stagnant sugar production. It also abolished the ecclesiastical tithes on imports. In response to the island's population crisis and lack of capital, immigration from friendly Roman Catholic countries was encouraged. The Crown developed a new policy of granting land to immigrants in proportion to the number of slaves they brought with them. Foreign ports were finally fully opened to the colony, ending Spain's monopoly of Puerto Rico's trade in agricultural products.[19]

The *Cédula de gracias* was a successful means of insuring Puerto Rico's allegiance to the Crown. It was not, however, the only reason for Puerto Rico's resurgent sugar industry. The end of the Haitian Revolution in 1804 effectively dismantled the sugar industry on Hispaniola. Puerto Rico, with its sister colony Cuba, filled the void left by Haiti's departure from the sugar industry. The increasing demand for sugar in the United States was another reason for Puerto Rico's rapid growth. The United States, with its ships and merchants, provided Puerto Rico with the means by which it could trade. Puerto Rico's nearby neighbor, the Dutch island of St. Thomas, offered Puerto Rico easy access to slaves and agricultural machinery for its emerging plantation-based economy. The abolition of the slave trade by Great Britain in 1820 led, in part, to the decline of sugar economies on neighboring islands. Illegal slaves cost more. Lastly, Spain's preoccupation with its war with Napoleon in Europe allowed Puerto Rico greater autonomy in its economic affairs.[20]

While Puerto Rico shared a slave-based labor pool with other plantation economies in the Caribbean, the Spanish colony displayed its own distinctive plantation system. One difference that set Puerto Rico's apart from the economies of the other islands was the participation of its subsistence or peasant farmers. Sugar production required accessible lowland soil for the planting of sugar cane. In Puerto Rico, with its central mountain range, such soil was found only in the coastal areas. This meant that sugar *haciendas* in Puerto Rico were established only in the coastal regions of the island, the largest ones being located on the western and southern coasts. The inland highlands were taken over by displaced peasant farmers who, using twice the amount of acreage cleared for growing sugarcane, grew coffee, and some tobacco, for export to European markets. Slave labor never was the dominant form of rural agriculture's work force in Puerto Rico.[21]

Another difference between Puerto Rico and the other sugar-producing economies was the relatively small size of its plantations. Puerto Rico never had the plantations of thousands of acres which were common in Cuba and Haiti.[22] With its narrow coastal strips of land, the highly efficient Puerto Rican plantations averaged sixty acres. These plantations were also often plagued by irrigation problems, soil erosion, and harsh weather.[23]

In Puerto Rico, again unlike plantations elsewhere in the Caribbean, plantation owners used fewer slaves. Sugarcane production was handled by an average of sixty slaves per plantation rather than the three or four hundred required by the huge plantations in other parts of the Caribbean.[24] In 1815 there were 19,000 slaves in Puerto

Rico. By 1828 the number grew to 32,000. Slave labor reached its peak at 42,000 in 1834.[25]

In addition to slave labor, the plantations always employed *jornaleros libres* (daily wage laborers) who worked side by side with the slaves. Slaves made up three quarters of a plantation's labor force, leaving the other quarter to be filled by *jornaleros libres*.[26] This practice was necessary, though not always welcomed by landowners due to the unreliability of free workers, in order to meet the labor demands required for high productivity.

The slave trade ended in 1820, and the local island government passed vagrancy laws in 1849. The *Libreta* (notebook) law required that laborers who had no means of subsistence had to work as day laborers, even if they owned land.[27] The day workers had to register their work in a notebook which they were required to carry with them at all times. In this notebook was recorded the worker's name, the name of the landowner, the name of the *hacienda*, and remarks by the landowner about how well the worker did his job.[28] This attempt at forced labor was ultimately unsuccessful. The *Libreta* laws were abolished in 1873, the same year slavery was abolished.

The sugar industry of Puerto Rico failed in the latter part of the nineteenth century due to multiple factors. The first was increasing competition. The production of sugar from sugar beets in Europe effectively eliminated Puerto Rico's Euorpean markets. Increasing production of raw sugar in Cuba and Louisiana cut into Puerto Rico's market in the United States, whose people at one time consumed seventy-five percent of Puerto Rico's *moscovado* (raw) sugar.[29] The second factor was the abolition of slavery in Puerto Rico. Abolition was the death knell for the island's sugar industry. By the 1880s, the number of *haciendas* had fallen by half.[30] Increasing competition in a world market

glutted with an abundant sugar supply, the cost of free labor
after emancipation, and heavy debt loads occasioned by
investments in costly steam-powered mills, led to the
decline and eventual end of Puerto Rico's status as a major
sugar producer.

CLASS AND COLOR

Class distinctions in Puerto Rico began with the
deeply-rooted division between the *peninsulares,* those free
people who were born on the Iberian peninsula, and the
criollos, those who were born on the island.[31]   The
peninsulares were the wealthy Spanish elite who had come
to the colony. They considered any form of manual labor,
particularly agricultural tasks, beneath them. Had they
wanted to do arduous work for a living, they could have
stayed home.   Their job, instead, was to surrender
themselves to the delights of this island paradise, while
slaves toiled in the fields.[32]

The *criollo's* lot, unlike that of the *peninsulare*, was to
farm for a living. This double indignity of having been
born without Iberian soil under one's feet, and with island
soil under one's fingernails, kept the *criollo* a second class
citizen. Only the slave was lower.

This fundamental dichotomy between · social
positions was at the heart of the class system and its
relationship to race as it developed in Puerto Rico. Slavery
was, in its origin in Puerto Rico, an economic rather than
a racial category.[33]   In the classic definition of slavery,
that a slave is the property of another, subject to the will
and authority of another, and whose work is obtained
through coercion by another,[34] the race of the slave is not
an essential consideration.[35]   Africans were enslaved in

Puerto Rico primarily out of what was perceived to be economic necessity, that is, the need for labor. The reasons were their social position (menial labor), their indigenous religions (pagan), and their color (black).[36] It must be added here, however, that black slaves in Puerto Rico were not seen by the Spaniards as a true metaphor for the devil as they were in British colonies. Instead, as in other parts of the Caribbean, their physical characteristics, black skin, "blubber" lips, and "flat" nose, were caricatured by the Spanish by turning the black slave into a "buffoon" or a "gargoyle."[37]

In the nineteenth century, with the immigration of upperclass whites from Spain, Hispaniola, and Europe to the island, this simple class system expanded, as did the society and the economy. Such immigrants brought with them capital and skills. Many of them were professional merchants, doctors, teachers, and administrators. Others bought land and became owners of large *haciendas.* Some, with their connections to European banking institutions, arranged the necessary financing that made international commerce in sugar possible.[38]

Small plantation owners and skilled workers made up the middle class. *Criollo* by birth, many of these Puerto Ricans were free *pardos* (mulattoes). They often had specialized skills that they put to work in jobs no white would take: shoemakers, blacksmiths, carpenters, iron-workers, and small shopkeepers.[39] These skills provided the necessary goods and services that kept the island's day-to-day economy running. The lower class was constituted by *agregados* (small peasant farmers), *jornaleros libres*, and slaves.

With their contempt for manual labor, the *peninsulares* judged a person, not so much by the color of his or her skin, as by the person's occupation. An individual's class was determined first by occupation and second by skin color. In reality, occupation and skin color tended to mirror each other. The reason for this primary emphasis on occupation was the numerous intermarriages between whites and blacks, as well as illicit liaisons, during the history of the colony. Racial mixing resulted in relatively few "pure" white families on the island. That is, there were few families without some black blood in their backgrounds.[40]

In addition to occupation and skin color, there was the wrinkle of adding yet another level to the class system: free or slave. For social purposes, free individuals whose parents were also free, were considered white. When free individuals got married, gave birth, or were buried, their names were entered into a "white" ecclesiastical register. Slave names were entered into a "black" Church record.[41] This nuance had particular ramifications for the free *pardos*. Generally speaking, *pardos* were considered to be neither white nor black because by definition they were born illegitimate, the fruit of relationships between white men and black slave women. This status, coupled with their status as manual laborers, led the whites to look upon the *pardos* as inferiors. There was also the threat of *pardos* being integrated into white society through years of "intermarrying" with whites. After many generations of marrying whites, it was possible for a *pardo's* family skin color to lighten.[42] In keeping with their Iberian status, whites clung to their social/color distinction both in general society and in the Church. The Church, of course, did not ordain blacks to the priesthood. It also did not ordain *pardos*.

From this outline we can see that a three-tiered class system developed during the first four hundred years of the colony. The whites were the dominant upperclass. The free *criollos* and free *pardos* made up the middle class. *Agregados, jornaleros libres,* and slaves were the lower class. *Jornaleros,* the individuals who were paid for their labor, were considered lower class because they were manual, unskilled laborers like slaves.

THE HACIENDA SYSTEM

The hacienda system in Puerto Rico, as distinct from small subsistence farming, shared certain characteristics with other plantation systems in the nineteenth century. Simply stated, unfree laborers were coerced into cultivating, harvesting, and processing a single crop, in this case sugar cane, for export to the benefit of the owners. *Haciendas,* then, relied chiefly on slaves as they were one crop agricultural producers, market-oriented and capitalistic.[43] In such an enterprise where profit depended upon, on the one hand, seemingly controllable factors such as labor and machinery and, on the other hand, unpredictable factors such as weather and fluctuating market prices, life on a *hacienda* was rigorous and often brutal for a slave.

On the *hacienda* there were three kinds of slaves: *doméstico, de tala,* and *jornaleros.* The *esclavos domésticos* were slaves who served in the house of the *hacendado* (*hacienda* owner) as domestic servants. The number of *domésticos* varied with the size of the house and its household. Their responsibilities included cooking and other typical household duties. The *esclavos de tala*[44] were slaves who worked in the fields. They worked from four in the morning until six at night. The *mayordomo* (foreman) was often a slave who was linked to the *hacendado* by blood. The slaves in the field obeyed his every command or suffered for their disobedience. The *esclavos jornaleros*, not to be confused with the *jornaleros libres*, were slaves who were rented out by the slaveowner to do work at other plantations.[45] This practice developed due to a shortage of labor and the high cost of *jornaleros libres*. The work done by the *escalvos jornaleros* often included the construction of roads, churche's, and fortifications as well as harvesting.[46]

The life of the *esclavos de tala* and the *esclavos jornaleros* centered on sugar production. There were three basic steps in sugar production: planting, harvesting, and processing, each with its own land, capital, and labor requirements. Planting sugarcane required many laborers because the work was done by hand. September planting had its own steps. Working in gangs, the laborers cleared the land and prepared it by digging irrigation ditches. Holes were then dug in straight rows into which seed canes were planted. The harvest began in January. Cane cutting required fewer laborers than planting, but this did not mean that some slaves and *jornaleros* were idle. The sugarcane had to be cut quickly and then delivered by oxcart to an *ingenio* (mill) on the plantation. After the cane was unloaded from the oxcarts, it was quickly crushed by the mill. Speed was necessary lest the moisture content in the cane evaporate. The harvest lasted for five months.[47]

In the milling process, the sugarcane stalks were put through a press which was either powered by horses, oxen, water, or steam. The press crushed the stalks, forcing the juice out of them. The juice was then boiled in order to remove any impurities. A boiling house was constructed on larger plantations solely for this purpose. The boiler ovens were fueled with sugarcane husks. After boiling, the sugarcane juice was brought to a purging house. There the sugar crystals were separated from the molasses in a refining process.[48]

Slaves were whipped, tortured, mutilated, and imprisoned as a way of correcting and coercing their behavior. These means of punishment were an integral part of Spanish law, and they were used extensively in the Spanish colonies.[49] To add insult to injury, the slaveowner did not dispense this harsh treatment himself. The *verdugo* (official executioner) was himself a slave. Sentences were carried out in public as a way of intimidating other slaves. The following list of punishments amply displays the barbaric use of force employed by the slaveowners to enforce their demands. The punishments a slave could expect for disobedience, stealing, attacking a slaveowner or overseer, fleeing, or rebelling included: *boca abajo*, tying a slave, face down, to four stakes and then applying the lash; *el cepo*, placing a slave in stocks to endure exposure; *el grillete,* shackling a slave to a wall by a chain connected to an iron collar around the neck; *la argolla,* placing a collar with iron spokes around a slave's neck to prohibit the slave from lying down comfortably; and *el mono*, loading an iron collar with three heavy weights. Other tortures included tying a slave to a horse's tail while the *verdugo* rode the horse; forcing a slave to eat fecal matter; coercing a slave woman to sleep with a male slave of exceptional strength and physique for the purpose of siring well-bred slave children; torturing a slave woman who refused the sexual advances of a slaveowner; and cutting off the eyelids of slave children so that they could not sleep while working in the fields during the harvest.[50] Many of these practices were eventually abolished in favor of imprisonment. Imprisonment was opposed by slaveowners due to the time the slave lost working in the fields. Any of the above tortures, including the cutting off of a slave's ears, did not prevent a slave from continuing to work.

In an effort to reduce the torture and trauma of slavery, the Spanish Crown and the Roman Catholic Church began regulating life on a *hacienda* in Puerto Rico. The *Real Orden* (Royal Order) of 1784 abolished the practice of *carimbo* (branding). This practice of branding slaves had begun with the Indian slaves during the conquest and colonization of the island. Prior to its abolition, each slave was branded on the shoulder with the letter "F", the monogram of Ferdinand, the King of Spain, as soon as he or she landed on the island.

In the *Codigo* (Code) of 1789 the Crown sought to protect the slaves from other abuses by their masters. This code required that masters provide their slaves with adequate food and shelter. The slave diet was an important consideration for slaveowners because adequate nourishment kept slaves strong. The diet consisted of plantains, potatoes, fish, rice, and fruits found on the island. During special occasions or illness, meat was provided. To augment meager provisions, slaves were given *conucos* (small plots of land) upon which they grew crops for their own consumption.[51]

The living quarters for slaves were located behind the master's house on the plantation. These quarters were of two kinds. For married slaves,[52] they were small enclosures made out of palm branches and leaves, reminiscent of the Taíno Indian *bohios* (huts). The slaves who were unmarried lived six to a barracks, separated by sex. In addition to food and housing, the slave owners also provided the slaves and their children with three sets of clothing each year, appropriate for the time of year. Infants were given several little shirts.[53]

The 1826 *Reglamento sobre la educacíon, trato, y ocupacíon que deben dar a sus esclavos los dueños y mayordomos de esta Isla* (Regulations concerning the education, treatment, and work that the owners and overseers should give to their slaves of this island) limited the hours per day a slave was allowed to work. During ordinary time, a slave was allowed to work only ten hours a day. At harvest time, the work day was increased to thirteen hours, leaving only eleven hours for rest and gardening.[54] Compliance with these orders, codes, and regulations was to be monitored by local district officials, and penalties were exacted from negligent and abusive masters. Not surprisingly, these laws were not scrupulously adhered to by slaveowners or officials.

The Roman Catholic Church had a twofold interest in the slaves. On the one hand, the Church argued for the acceptability, even the necessity, of slavery while simultaneously condemning its abuses. On the other hand, the Church desired to convert the slaves to Christianity. The ownership of *esclavos domésticos* by many of the Roman Catholic clergy in Puerto Rico demonstrated the Church's approval of the institution of slavery. The Church's partnership with the Spanish Crown, as well as the Church's moral stance, allowed the Church a free hand in censuring intolerable slave conditions while not calling for slavery's abolition. The Church accomplished this contradiction by appealing to the need to meet the spiritual and religious needs of the slaves. This meant converting the slaves to Christianity with the help of the slaveowners.

Conversion to Christianity included not only the adherence to Roman Catholic beliefs and the practice of Roman Catholic rituals. It also involved conformity to a life of respect for, and obedience to, the slave's superiors. Conversion in both forms was to insure the order and tranquility of the colony as well as the salvation of the soul. This process of conversion began as soon as the slave arrived on the island. Church law dictated that each slave owner was responsible for the catechesis of each slave for a period of one year. During this time each slave was to be taught the basic tenets of the faith including the creed, the articles of faith, the "Our Father," the Ten Commandments, and the sacraments of the Church. When this was accomplished, the slave was baptized.[55]

The Church also insisted that slaves were not to work on Sundays and feast days. These days were for hearing mass and receiving communion.[56] Feast days were especially important. These days were not only religious holidays; they were times of recreation for the slaves. In a fiesta for a saint, the Church mixed religious observance with entertainment. The fiestas began at three o'clock in the afternoon and ended at sundown, the Church's designated time for evening prayer by all. Everyone from the *hacienda* and the town joined in the festivities. The slaves sang songs about their African past and feasted on special foods, drinks, and sweets. The highlight of the fiesta was the *bailes de bomba*, African-based dances accompanied by *tamboriles* (drums), *cuatros* (Spanish inspired four-string guitars), and *güiros* (Taíno Arawak Indian musical instruments made out of guords which when scratched made a rasping sound). The whites, free blacks, and free mulattos danced together. The games included *juego de pelota,* a ball game similar to today's soccer.[57]

Not only religious observances and forms of recreation, the fiestas were designed as both catechesis and a means of solidifying the slaves into a community under the guidance of the Church and the rule of the slaveowner. A community of slaves took the form of a *cofradía* (fraternity) or *hermandad* (brotherhood), groupings also used by whites and *pardos*. Each fraternity grew up around a patron saint whose feast day was the most important day of the year for that group.[58] The slave *cofradías* also served a purpose that was wholly unintended by the Church and the slaveowner. In addition to assimilating the slaves into the Church, these fraternities generated a spirit of freedom. This is most clearly seen in a fiesta's most common dance, the *baile de bomba*. The *baile de bomba* became known as "the dance of conspiracy" by slaveowners.[59] In the sound of the drums and the dance movements remembered from Africa, the slaves found a means by which they could externalize their spirit for rebellion. And since each fraternity came together with other fraternities during a fiesta for a saint, the fiesta itself became a mask for planning rebellion. The slaves took advantage of their free time during the fiesta to conspire together against their slaveowners. This practice became so prevalent that fiestas had to regulated by the government.[60]

SLAVE CONSPIRACIES AND REBELLIONS

Although it was relatively peaceful in the early part of the nineteenth century, Puerto Rico experienced some small uprisings on its plantations in the years between 1826 and 1841. After 1841 the slave insurrections were much more serious. There are three reasons for this change. First, most of the insurrections during this period were led by *bozales,* those slaves who had recently arrived from Africa, making them more resistant to slavery than those who had been on the plantations longer. Second, news of the successful slave revolution in Haiti had made its way to Puerto Rico. Coupled with talk about abolishing slavery on the island, Haiti's independence aroused a hope for liberty

among Puerto Rico's slave population. Third, during the
1840s, the sugar industry in Puerto Rico was in decline.
Fluctuating sugar prices in the world markets, droughts,
high export tariffs, and a scarcity of slaves due to their
enormous cost, gave the slaves even more work to do than
before. Landowners, in an effort to minimize their growing
losses, annexed the land which the slaves had used for their
own subsistence farming. The landowners also severely
limited the rest time and days off for fiestas because of the
need to farm the land. With this added burden, the slaves
faced exhaustion.[61]

These rebellions were often planned during the
Church's feast days. The feast days, with their fiestas, gave
the slaves an opportunity to gather as a group. During the
bailes de bomba (African dances), they used the fiestas as
a disguise while they plotted against their masters. The
slave revolts were carefully planned. Sometimes the
planning took several months. The slaves took into
consideration the strength of their opposition, where the
arms were stored, and the geography of the region.[62] The
plan of attack usually took the form of the slaves setting
fire to the sugarcane fields. With their machetes, they then
killed those who came out into the fields to douse the blaze.
When this was accomplished, the slaves returned to the
hacienda in order to capture the munitions depot. They
needed the arms to fight off the *milicia urbana* which was
called upon to hunt them down.[63] Sometimes the revolts
were designed only to kill the *mayordomo* (overseer).

Major uprisings took place in Bayamón (1821),
Ponce (1841 and 1848), and Toa Baja (1843). These, and
some forty other uprisings, did not often succeed because
slaves informed the overseer or the slaveowner of the
conspiracy. This led to the eventual capture and
punishment of the rebellious slaves. The informant was

rewarded with money. The conspirators were rewarded with death. Some individual slaves rebelled against slavery by choosing to flee rather than fight. Like those slaves who revolted, fugitives rarely escaped capture and punishment. They were quickly caught because their description was advertised in the *Gaceta Oficial de Puerto Rico* (Official Government Journal of Puerto Rico) until they were captured.[64]

Two laws promulgated during this period also made an escape from slavery difficult. The *Reglamento de Esclavos* (Regulations Concerning Slaves) of 1826 was intended to protect the slaveowners from their slaves. It did so by putting into practice several precautionary restrictions on slave behavior. First, the *Reglamento* made clear that rebellious slaves would be severely punished. Second, it ordered slaveowners to lock up at night the agricultural implements used during the day by the field slaves. This meant that the slaves no longer had access to their machetes. Third, the times and places where slaves could rest were strictly circumscribed. Since uprisings were frequently planned under the darkness of night, a light was kept on in the slave quarters throughout the night. Guards were positioned to listen for conversation among slaves. Fourth, the *Reglamento* prohibited slaves from one plantation visiting another plantation without permission and an escort. This prevented slaves from many plantations collaborating in an insurrection. Moreover, any slaveowner could detain an unknown slave caught on his property, jail that slave, and demand a fine from the slave's owner.[65]

This particular injunction had interesting ramifications for fiestas. Fiestas had to take place only on the plantation grounds and in an open space visible to the watchful eyes of the slaveowner or overseer. In addition, the sexes were separated during the fiesta, alcohol use outlawed, and free blacks, sympathetic to the cause of freedom, were banned from speaking with slaves. Finally, the law promised liberty or a reward to any slave who informed the slaveowner about any conspiracy to rebel.[66]

The *Bando Contra la Raza Africana* (Edict Against the African Race) of 1848 added another element to the protection of the slaveowners on the island. This decree stated that there would be no distinction made between free Africans and slaves or their descendents. All would be punished for rebellious activity without regard for their legal status because they were all black. This decree reaffirmed, in all cases, the superiority of whites over blacks in Puerto Rico. It stated that any aggression against a white by a black, whether by words or by weapons, was punishable by whipping, incarceration, mutilation, or death. Each case would be judged by the *Consejo de Guerra* (the military court of law) and punished by the military.[67]

Rather than revolt or flee, there were four legal ways a slave might obtain freedom short of the abolition of slavery. A slave could purchase freedom through *coartación*. *Coartación* was a legal right granted to slaves which guaranteed that a slave could pay the slaveowner a fixed price, little by little if necessary, to purchase his or her freedom. This guarantee was designed to reduce the danger of slave uprisings.[68] During the precarious times of the nineteenth century, this right was sharply curtailed.

Manumission, the granting of freedom by the slaveowner to the slave at no cost, sometimes occurred upon the death of the slaveowner. In his last will and testament, the slaveowner manumitted the slave as an offering to God, in hopes that those left behind, being moved by his generosity, would pray for the salvation of his eternal soul. Other instances of manumission occurred when a slave showed exceptional service, as in revealing a conspiracy against the slaveowner, or when a slave was affectionate to the slaveowner and his family, was of advanced age, or was very ill. Occasionally, the slaveowner also manumitted his slave mistress and her illegitimate children.[69]

PUERTO RICO IN THE TWENTIETH CENTURY

It is not within the scope of this study to describe in detail the political, economic, and social complexities of Puerto Rico's history. A brief outline of the significant events and trends that still shape life on the island today will have to suffice as additional background to the fiesta for St. James the Apostle in Loíza Aldea. In 1898, the same year in which the United States invaded the island, Puerto Rico had successfully negotiated its independence, ending five centuries of Spanish colonial rule. The United States invaded Puerto Rico because it needed a military foothold in the Caribbean. To insure its control of the island, the United States's legislature passed the Foraker Act in 1900. This act gave the President of the United States total power in appointing the governor of the island.

A series of political, economic, and social changes over the past several decades have been attempted by the United States government to soften its domination of the island. The results have been to some a disguise for colonialism, that is, Puerto Rico's nearly complete dependence upon the United States. To others, Puerto Rico stands as "the shining star of the Caribbean,"[70] a model of stability, democracy, and economic growth in the region. These attempts at softening the grip of the United States on Puerto Rico began with the Jones Act of 1917. This act granted all Puerto Ricans United States citizenship.

Although they had no vote in general elections and no representation in Washington D.C., young Puerto Rican males were required to register for the draft.

The first Puerto Rican to be elected governor of the island, Luis Muñoz Marín, took office in 1947. In 1952, the island was officially recognized as a Commonwealth, or a "free associated state," with limited political autonomy. This status granted Puerto Rico its own government which was modeled after that of the United States. The rights of the Federal government with regard to the island were also legitimized. The Federal government retained its role in determining the island's foreign relations, defense, postal system, and customs service. In 1967, a plebiscite on the political status of the island revealed that only 6 percent of the island's population openly desired independence from the United States. Sixty percent favored Commonwealth status. The remainder voted for statehood. In 1993 another plebiscite showed that the proponents of statehood were making some headway. Forty-six percent of the island's inhabitants voted for statehood, narrowly losing to the forty-eight percent who voted to remain a commonwealth. As before, the votes for independence were meager.

Economically, Puerto Rico used to be an island that depended on agriculture and fishing. With the U.S. invasion, this changed dramatically. With large sugar and tobacco corporations monopolizing most of the best land, and the United States navy controlling the coastal waters, agriculture and fishing have still not recovered. One result has been chronic unemployment and a country which does not produce that which its people consume.[71] Puerto Rico now imports 80 percent of its goods from the United States. In this capacity, Puerto Rico is second only to Canada.

In the 1940s, the island government encouraged a mass migration from the island to the United States as a way of easing the unemployment crisis. "Operation Bootstrap," an effort at promoting increased productivity, jobs, and a higher standard of living, began in the 1950s. This initiative was focused on attracting large petrochemical and pharmaceutical companies to the island in exchange for cheap labor, tax incentives[72], deep water ports, and loose environmental controls. Along with the United States' naval maneuvers, chemical pollution has greatly damaged the fishing waters. Although some Puerto Rican citizens no doubt benefited, unemployment did not decrease. The 1960s saw the introduction of the American welfare system, especially its emphasis on food stamps, to the island as a way of propping up Puerto Rico's severely ailing economy. The economic recession of the mid-1970s exacerbated Puerto Rico's enduring problems of unemployment, and its attendant results, poor housing and a substandard of living for many. The 1980s brought a new emphasis to the island. Service-sector jobs as well as tourism were seen as the wave of the future, but progress has stalled. The island is still hampered by 18 percent unemployment and half of the population received some kind of assistance from the federal government.[73]

In addition to Puerto Rico's political problems and economic hardships, the island's social problems are seen by some as a direct result of Puerto Rico's militarization and Americanization. The island houses two major United States naval bases. One, Roosevelt Roads, is on the south coast of the island. The other, off the east coast on Vieques, virtually consumes the entirety of the small island. Americanization began with the invasion. It took three forms: the enforcement of the English language in schools, the campaign of Protestant missionaries against the "superstitions" of Roman Catholicism, and the replacement of Spanish law by American jurisprudence. Although these attempts at Americanization appear to have failed, the pressures to participate in the American "way of life," its commercialization and conspicuous consumption appear to be growing.[74]

Since the invasion in 1898, protests against the American presence on the island have appeared from time to time. Sometimes they have been violent. Three battles stand out: the Río Piedras Massacre (1935), the Ponce Massacre (1937), and the Rebellion of 1950. Today's protestors may come from the *Macheteros*, a group of *independentistas* who believe that Puerto Rico can regain its freedom only through armed conflict. Most recently, two young independence activists were murdered by police in 1978 at Cerro Maravilla. Not until 1983 did the facts regarding their death, and its subsequent cover-up by local authorities, come to public awareness.

LOIZA ALDEA

Loíza Aldea's story is in many ways a microcosm of the history described in this chapter. At the time of the conquest, it was the site of a *yucayeque* (Taíno Indian village) in a region called *Jaymanio* with *Yiayza* as its *cacica* (female chief). Her name was changed to *Luisa* upon her baptism. She is famous in the early stories of Puerto Rico as a woman who did not seek her own safety in a time of grave danger. She did not leave her Spanish mulatto husband, Francisco Mexia, when her people were attacked by Caribes. Both *Luisa* and her husband were killed in the attack. Her story tells us that she died in her husband's arms.

Loíza Aldea was one of the early locations where the Spaniards searched for gold on the island of *San Juan*

Bautista (St. John the Baptist), Spain's original name for Puerto Rico. The Spaniards forced the indigenous Taíno Arawak Indians to mine the *Río Grande de Loíza*. By 1519 slaves were brought to Loíza Aldea to aid in the mining. When the gold deposits ran out, slaves worked with subsistence farmers in the earliest cultivation of sugarcane on the island. By 1581 Loíza Aldea had three mills in operation. In 1690 the village (*aldea*) of Loíza was created, and later, in 1719, it was officially recognized. The oldest parish church on the island, *la iglesia de San Patricio* (the church of St. Patrick), was built during this period. An early *partido*, Loíza Aldea's people defended the island from attacks by the Caribes in the sixteenth century, the Dutch in the seventeenth, and the British in the eighteenth.

By the middle of the eighteenth century Loíza Aldea had the highest concentration of blacks on the island. When sugar production dramatically increased on the island in the first half of the nineteenth century, Loíza Aldea participated in the boom as evidenced by its three *haciendas*. These *haciendas* were owned and controlled by Irish immigrants.[75] With the demise of the sugar industry in the middle of the nineteenth century, the local population was made up of mostly free blacks and mulattos. Sugar production again changed radically after the United States invaded the island in 1898. By 1910 sugar firms in the United States controlled more than 62 percent of the land cleared for sugar production. Workers were paid salaries and production was highly mechanized in this new system called *centrales*, that produced a finer grade of sugar.[76] With mechanization came unemployment since fewer workers were required to run the machines.

One of the most important *centrales* on the island was *La Central de Canóvanas (de Loíza)*. When it closed in 1960, Loíza Aldea was thrown into an economic crisis.

Those who did not find jobs in the cities returned to subsistence farming in sugarcane and coconuts. Some fished. By 1970, 90 percent of the population in Loíza Aldea were at the poverty level with 84 percent relying on food stamps. In 1982, the rate of unemployment among Loiceños was estimated at 27.7 percent, with unemployment among the village's youth estimated to be as high as 54 percent. With the ongoing problems of inadequate housing, lack of medical facilities, alcoholism, and a youthful population in need of education (88 percent of the population in 1970 were between the ages of 5 and 44 years old), meant that Loíza Aldea had great problems indeed.[77] The answer, thus far, has been welfare.

Due to its geographical isolation and racial characteristics, Loíza Aldea has not benefited from the industrialization of the island. In spite of the hardships which it has endured, Loíza Aldea remains well-known on the island as a village which maintains its Indian, African, and Spanish traditions, traditions intermingled during Puerto Rico's history. Its most famous tradition, the fiesta of Santiago Apóstol, is the focus for our discussion in the following chapters.

NOTES

1. Don Castor Ayala, the premier mask maker of Loíza Aldea, gave Henrietta Yurchenco this date for the beginning of the fiesta in an interview included in her book, ¡Hablamos! Puerto Ricans Speak (New York: Praeger Publishers, 1971), 42,50.

2. Luis González Vales, "Towards a Plantation Society," in Puerto Rico: A Political and Cultural History, ed. Arturo Morales Carrión (New York: W.W. Norton & Co., Inc., 1983), 103.

3. The other areas were Arecibo, Toa Baja, Bayamón, Río Piedras, Trujillo, Farjardo, Añasco, San Germán, Yauco, and Patillas, with Mayagüez, Ponce, and Guayama being the largest. Loíza Aldea was among the smallest. See Francisco A. Scarano, *Sugar and Slavery in Puerto Rico: The Plantation Economy of Ponce, 1800-1850* (Madison: The University of Wisconsin Press, 1984), 17.

4. Gordon K. Lewis, *Main Currents in Caribbean Thought: The Historical Evolution of Caribbean Society in Its Ideological Aspects, 1492-1900* (Baltimore: The Johns Hopkins University Press, 1983), 10.

5. The Spaniards "discovered" the island of Borinquén (Puerto Rico) in 1493. The enslavement of the indigenous Indians began in 1508 with the arrival of Juan Ponce de Leon, the island's first governor. Some black slaves came to the island as early as 1507 according to Eugenio Fernández Méndez, *Las Encomiendas y Esclavitud de los Indios de Puerto Rico, 1508-1550*, Quinta edición (Río Piedras, Puerto Rico: Editorial Universitaria-Universidad de Puerto Rico, 1976), 55.

6. David Brion Davis, *The Problem of Slavery in Western Culture* (Ithaca, New York: Cornell University Press, 1966), 102.

7. Eric Williams, *From Columbus to Castro: The History of the Caribbean 1492-1969* (London: André Deutsch, Limited, 1970), 30.

8. Jalil Sued Badillo y Angel López Cantos, *Puerto Rico Negro* (Río Piedras, Puerto Rico: Editorial Cultural, 1986), 139.

9. Herbert S. Klein, *African Slavery in Latin America and the Caribbean* (New York: Oxford University Press, 1986), 218.

10. *Ladinos* were slaves brought from Spain where they had lived for at least one year. During that year they were inculturated into Spanish life and Christian beliefs.

11. Williams, 28.

12. Aida R. Caro Costas, "The Organization of an Institutional and Social Life," in *Puerto Rico: A Political and Cultural History*, ed. Arturo Morales Carrión (New York: W.W. Norton and Co., Inc., 1983), 32.

13. Aida R. Caro Costas, "The Outpost of Empire," in Morales Carrión, 24.

14. Sidney W. Mintz, *Caribbean Transformations* (Chicago: Aldine Publishing Co., 1974), 87.

15. Klein, 221, and Scarano, 41.

16. Klein, 236.

17. *Ibid.*, 222.

18. Mintz, 85.

19. Scarano, 18.

20. *Ibid.*, 22.

21. Klein, 104.

22. Scarano, 63.

23. *Ibid.*, 47.

24. Klein, 107.

25. *Ibid.*, 106.

26. *Ibid.*, 107.

27. Andrés A. Ramos Mattei, "Technical Innovations and Social Change in the Sugar Industry of Puerto Rico, 1870-1880," in *Between Slavery and Free Labor: The Spanish-Speaking Caribbean in the Nineteenth Century*, eds. Manuel Moreno Fraginals, Frank Moya Pons, and Stanley

L. Engerman (Baltimore: The Johns Hopkins University Press, 1985), 159.

28. José Curet, "About Slavery and the Order of Things: Puerto Rico, 1845-1873," in Moreno Fraginals, *et. al.*, 120.

29. Scarano, 9.

30. Klein, 105.

31. Manuel Maldonado-Denis, *Puerto Rico: A Socio-Historic Interpretation*, trans. Elena Vialo (New York: Random House, 1972), 22-23.

32. Luis M. Díaz Soler, *Historia de la Esclavitud en Puerto Rico* (Río Piedras, Puerto Rico: Editorial Universitaria-Universidad de Puerto Rico, 1981), 147.

33. Lewis, 95.

34. Davis, 31.

35. Lewis, 95.

36. *Ibid.*, 98.

37. Lemuel A. Johnson, *The Devil, the Gargoyle, and the Buffoon: The Negro as Metaphor in Western Literature* (Port Washington, New York: National University Publications, Kennikat Press, 1971), 19-20.

38. Scarano, 87-97.

39. Sued Badillo y López Cantos, 272.

40. *Ibid.*, 259.

41. *Ibid.*, 260-261.

42. *Ibid.*, 273.

43. Mintz, 96.

44. *Tala* literally means "felling of trees."

45. Díaz Soler, 150-154.

46. Sued Badillo y López Cantos, 165.

47. Scarano, 100-102.

48. *Ibid.*, 105-110.

49. *Ibid.*, 162.

50. Díaz Soler, 184-185.

51. *Ibid.*, 161.

52. In actuality, very few slave "marriages" were sanctioned by the Church. To the Church's consternation, these relationships were popularly sanctioned.

53. Díaz Soler, 163-166.

54. *Ibid.*, 153.

55. *Ibid.*, 169.

56. During harvest time, this practice was suspended.

57. *Ibid.*, 175-176.

58. Sued Badillo y López Cantos, 291-292.

59. Guillermo A. Baralt, *Esclavos Rebeldes: Conspiraciones y Sublevaciones de Esclavos en Puerto Rico (1795-1873)* (Río Piedras, Puerto Rico: Ediciones Huracán, 1985), 59.

60. *Ibid.*, 174.

61. *Ibid.*, 171-172.

62. *Ibid.*, 172.

63. *Ibid.*, 174.

64. *Ibid.*, 158.

65. *Ibid.*, 68-79.

66. *Ibid.*, 70-71.

67. *Ibid.*, 130.

68. Davis, 266.

69. Sued Badillo y López Cantos, 300-301.

70. This is the slogan used by the Tourism Company of the Commonwealth of Puerto Rico to describe the island to tourists.

71. "Inside Puerto Rico 1984: Colonialism and Intervention in the Caribbean and Central America," *Prisa International: Publication of the National Ecumenical Movement of Puerto Rico (PRISA)* 7 (April 1984): 9.

72. This refers chiefly to Section 936 of the Internal Revenue Code which allows United States' companies to shelter the profits they gain from their subsidiaries in Puerto Rico. The Congress of the United States has voted to begin reducing these benefits beginning in 1994.

73. Laurence I. Barrett, "Puerto Rico: State of Anticipation," *Time*, 8 November 1993, 48.

74. Raymond Carr, *Puerto Rico: A Colonial Experiment* (New York: Vintage Books, 1984), 279-289.

75. Ricardo E. Alegría, *La Fiesta de Santiago Apóstol en Loíza Aldea* (San Juan, Puerto Rico: Colección de Estudios Puertorriqueños, 1954), 3.

76. David L. Ungerlieder Kepler, *Fiestas Afro-Borincanas y Cambio Social en Puerto Rico: El Caso de Loíza*, M.A. Thesis (Mexico: Escuela Nacional de Antropología e Historia, 1983), 57.

77. *Ibid.*, 60-63.

3

THE FIESTA OF SANTIAGO APOSTOL

INTRODUCTION

The old saying "lex orandi, lex credendi"[1] may be translated as "what you worship shows what you believe." This is the theological viewpoint. In anthropological terms the emphasis shifts to "what you worship shows who you are." The fiesta[2] of Santiago Apóstol in Loíza Aldea is a "liturgy of the streets." It is a "public work of the people." Viewed from an anthropological perspective, the fiesta shows who the people of Loíza Aldea are. It brings out into the open "the private works" of the village's social structure.[3] The private is made public through the ritual process of inversion. The focus of this process is Santiago Apóstol, the patron saint of Loíza Aldea. When his three statues are paraded through the streets of the village, he symbolically dislocates himself from the social structure. This dislocation symbolizes the neutralization of the differences which separate the people and define the village. Santiago Apóstol symbolizes, then, not how life is, but how it should be.

Life as it is is symbolized by the masked figures of the fiesta, the ritual clowns. They, too, mimic the social structure, but their mimicry is of a different sort. Rather than neutralize the differences among the people, they accentuate them through parody. Their concentration on the

55

reality of the social structure is not a direct one, however. It is masked, disguised by their costumes and actions. Unlike the statues of the saint, the masked figures do not simply cross a boundary, they stand on the boundary.[4] They have one foot in the social structure and another foot in the liminal space that suspends it.

The ritual clowns, along with the saint and the people of Loíza Aldea, are the major characters in the fiesta of Santiago Apóstol. All of them take part in the passage of the religious processions. The saint represents *communitas*.[5] The ritual clowns, as we will see more clearly in the next chapter, represent the meeting of the social structure and its critique. The people, by their participation in the religious processions, reveal to themselves the social structure that they have been concealing. It is interesting to note that whenever I have asked the villagers about the ritual clowns, I have been told one of three things: the legend of *Santiago Matamoros,* the story of the discovery of the original statue, or how the clowns have been traditionally dressed. All of these comments are rooted in the past. No contemporary commentary is ever offered. Moreover, whereas the people seem drawn to the statues of the saint, I sense an ambivalence regarding the ritual clowns. Except for the *caballero,* who represents the saint, the other three ritual clowns, the *vejigante* (devil), the *viejo* (old man), and the *loca* (crazy woman), are regarded with varying levels of discomfort or amusement. I attribute these reactions to the fact that the reality of the ritual clowns is much closer to the reality of the people than is the saint.

In the symbolic dislocations which occur in the religious processions, social conflicts are handled by temporarily inverting the social structures. The saint is "uncrowned" and the ritual clowns gain authority. This inversion allows a social space for calling into question their givenness. This process of questioning, though short lived, can be seen as one of the reasons, albeit a hidden one, for the fiesta and its celebrations. The religious processions are a "time out" from the religious convictions imposed by the Church, from the local history that repeats itself in the present, from the racial differences that characterize Puerto Ricans, and from the social relationships which separate and divide the village. However, with the end of the fiesta, none of the social structures has actually been changed, none of the conflicts has been resolved. On the contrary, they are reinforced. We will see examples of this when we look at the ritual clowns in detail.

The religious processions, the liturgies of the streets, are the primary context for the appearance of Santiago Apóstol in public. It is necessary, then, to discuss these processions in some detail. In our analysis of them, we will learn what they have to say about the people of Loíza Aldea.

ROOTS

The fiesta of Santiago Apóstol is rooted in the long Roman Catholic tradition of patronal festivals held to honor the Church's saints and martyrs. As early as the second century the Church honored those individuals and fraternities who witnessed to Christ at the cost of their own lives by gathering on the anniversary of the martyr's death, and when possible, at the site of burial. By the third century the burial dates for martyrs became feast days, the holy days of commemoration which can be found throughout the Church's liturgical year. With the conversion of Emperor Constantine in the fourth century, the feast days became popular holidays and their number grew.

These holy feast days became popular because of the conviction that death did not separate the martyr from Christ.[6] It only brought the martyr, as a resident of heaven, closer to Christ. The martyr, then, could be called on to intercede with Christ on behalf of the supplicant. This practice of praying for intercession gradually evolved into asking the martyr directly for help, bypassing Christ. Often included in the supplicant's prayer was a promise to give the martyr something in return for his or her aid. In the Middle Ages, this return frequently took the form of a pilgrimage to the holy burial place of the martyr. After an often long, arduous, and dangerous journey, the pilgrim arrived at a shrine or church where he or she could take part in religious processions, listen to speeches recalling the good deeds of the martyr, and venerate powerful sacred relics such as the bones, hair, or clothing of the martyr.[7]

One such martyr was St. James the Apostle. With the reconquest of Spain, he became its patron saint and was honored with a shrine at Compostela in northwest Spain. In the eleventh and twelfth centuries, Compostela became one of the most popular pilgrimage sites along with Jerusalem and Rome.

It must be noted, however, that the original patron of Loíza Aldea was St. Patrick. In 1645 a plague of ants ravaged the *yuca* crop. When the people of the village asked the priest for a saint who could protect the crop, the priest put some names into a box. Then the priest put his hand into the box three times to pull out a name. Each time the name which appeared was that of St. Patrick. After a *novena* in honor of St. Patrick, the plague stopped. This miracle made St. Patrick the protector of *yuca*. When Irish immigrants gained control of the larger *haciendas* in

Loíza Aldea in the nineteenth century, they gave an image of St. Patrick, the patron saint of Ireland, to the church. In turn, the priest named the church after the saint. The people of the village, however, adopted the patron of Spain, Santiago Apóstol, as their own for three reasons. First, St. Patrick's feast day fell within the liturgical season of Lent, a season without celebrations. Second, St. Patrick bore no resemblance to the Yoruba god, Shangó. And third, in the early part of the nineteenth century, a statue of Santiago Apóstol miraculously appeared in a tree trunk in the village.[8]

The Legend of St. James the Apostle

For several centuries Catholic Spain was occupied by the Moors. Into this scene came the figure of Santiago Apóstol or St. James the Apostle.[9] A martyr for the new faith, St. James was beheaded in 44 A.D. by King Herod Agrippa. This Galilean fisherman, with St. Peter, was called "Son of Thunder" by Christ, presumably for his impatience and fiery temper.

As Santiago Apóstol, St. James the Apostle is a watershed figure in Spanish history. Legend has it that Santiago Apóstol traveled to Spain preaching the Gospel. During the Moorish occupation,[10] the legend continues, the bones of Santiago Apóstol were dug up in Galicia, near Compostela, after being miraculously transported there from Jerusalem, the traditional place of his martyrdom. In the early decades of the ninth century, perhaps about 814, Bishop Teodomiro of Iria (Padrón), learned that a hermit living near the River Sar had been told by angels that St. James was buried in a forest nearby. A star shone over the site day and night. The Bishop went to the site, cleared

away the trees, and found the ruins of a building, a small
courtyard with two graves, and a small chapel atop a crypt
of a third grave. This third grave Bishop Teodomiro
proclaimed as the burial site of St. James. The site was
called *Campo de la Estrella*, the field of the star. Its name
eventually be *came Compostela*. Upon hearing of the event,
Alfonso II of Spain visited the site and declared Santiago to
be the protector of Spain.[11] The importance of Santiago's
transformation from apostle to protector is made clear in the
context of the *Reconquista*.

Before a battle in which Santiago Apóstol is
believed to have appeared, the reconquest was little more
than a series of skirmishes. That all changed in 844 at the
battle of Clavijo when the Spanish king Ramiro I led a
small band of men against the Moors after his troops were
nearly decimated in an earlier ambush. T. D. Kendrick tells
the story of Santiago's appearance this way:

> The surviving Spaniards escaped into the hills and
> took refuge under the crag of Clavijo. Night fell, and
> then a wonderful thing happened. St. James appeared
> to the sleeping king in a dream and announced that he
> had been specially commissioned by Jesus Christ to
> take Spain under his protection, and to prove at once
> the advantages to the Spaniards of this appointment,
> he went on to promise Ramiro victory on the
> following day in a battle in which the apostle said he
> himself would take part. The king was assured that
> the casualties on the Christian side would be almost
> negligible, and that in any case the fallen would rank
> as martyrs, each one being destined to receive a well-
> deserved crown in heaven. Ramiro listened
> attentively to this ghostly encouragement, and when
> morning came, after the confessions, masses, and
> communions ordered by St. James had all been
> devoutly performed, the Christians, now in good

heart, descended into the plain and the famous battle
of Clavijo began. And St. James appeared at the head
of the Spanish army, visible to all, as he had
promised, and so inspired the Spaniards that the
Moors were hopelessly overwhelmed and routed.
About 70,000 of the infidels were killed. It was in
this wonderful victory, so Ramiro said, that the
Spanish army used for the first time the battle-cry
Adjuva nos Deus et Jacobe. May God and St. James
come to our aid![12]

When a powerful and wealthy Spain ventured forth
into the New World in the late fifteenth century, it brought
Santiago Apóstol with it. The cry against the Moors, "Dios
ayuda y Santiago", was often heard in the West Indies as
the Spaniards fought against those who would be her first
slaves in the New World, the Taíno Arawak Indians. With
the cross-emblazoned banner of Santiago Apóstol in one
hand and a sword in the other, the Spaniards were again
victorious.

Origins of the Fiesta

Each year the villagers of Loíza Aldea, Puerto Rico
celebrate for ten days the July 25th feast of their patron, St.
James the Apostle. During this celebration the villagers
remember the old tale brought to the New World by the
Conquistadores (Conquerors) of how the Spaniards routed
the Moors with the help of St. James, the *Matamoros*
(Moorslayer). They also remember the help given to the
settlers and slaves of Loíza Aldea by St. James the Apostle
when, in the early years of the settlement, he aided them in

defending their shores from frequent assaults by their neighbors, the fierce Caribe Indians.

It is uncertain when this festival honoring St. James first became a part of Loíza Aldea's yearly celebration. Some say that the celebration is as old as the time "when the gods walked the earth." A traditional story about the discovery of the original statue of Santiago Apóstol suggests a possible dating. The story tells how an old woman found a statue in a tree trunk in the Medianías[13] around the year 1832.[14] She showed the statue to the local priest who believed that it was an icon of Santiago Apóstol. He installed the statue in the local church. The next day the same statue was found back in its original place, the tree trunk. The priest brought the statue back to the church and, declaring that a miracle had taken place, began the yearly celebration. He said a mass and led a procession from the tree trunk to the church and around the town plaza. This tradition remains virtually intact today.[15]

As in many other places in the Caribbean and Latin America, slaves brought their own spirits or gods to the altars of the Spaniards. These spirits were later conflated with the Christian saints. In the case of the Taíno Indians in Puerto Rico, a shift took place. The Taíno Indian representation of a spirit, the *cemi*, fashioned out of clay, wood, gold or stone became the *santo*, a wooden carving of a saint.[16]

The African slaves followed a similar pattern. Although done differently in other places in the Caribbean, one example of this pattern was the fusion of *Santiago Matamoros* with Ogun and Shangó,[17] two warrior spirits among the Yoruba people of West Africa. The spirit of war, Ogun, and the spirit of thunder and lightening, Shangó, found a kindred spirit in *Santiago Matamoros*. Like them, this Christian warrior-saint was a "Son of Thunder" who

hurled bolts of lightning down from the heavens to destroy
his enemies. The god *Shangó* is associated with thunder and
lightning. One myth about him tells us about his closeness
to thunder.

> Once upon a time ... Shangó was recklessly
> experimenting with a leaf that had the power to bring
> down lightning from the skies and inadvertantly
> caused the roof of the palace of Oyo to be set afire
> by lightning. In the blaze his wife and children were
> killed. Half crazed with grief and guilt, Shangó went
> to a spot outside the royal capital and hanged himself
> from the branches of an ayan tree. He thus suffered
> the consequences of playing arrogantly with God's
> fire, and became lightning itself.[18]

The result of this story is that *Shangó*

> ...became an eternal moral presence, rumbling in the
> clouds, outraged by impure human acts, targeting the
> homes of adulterers, liars, and thieves for
> destruction.[19]

Another important god in the Yoruba pantheon is
Ogun. *Ogun* is a "hot" god associated with war and iron.
He is the one who clears pathways for others to travel.
With his machete he cuts down enemies on the battlefields,
cuts through a forest to clear a road, and cuts into a
farmer's soil for planting. The Yoruba view him as an
indispensable god because he cleared the way for the other
gods to descend to earth.[20] He also is said to have cut
through the primordial forest, creating the sixteen paths by
which the sixteen sons of the first king of Ile-Ife traveled
to their kingdoms.[21]

THE TRADITION

The Organization of the Fiesta

The organization of the fiesta[22] for Santiago
Apóstol belongs to the *matenadoras* (guardians of the
statues). Usually women, the *matenadoras* look after the
statues of the saint as if they were their own. If a
matenadora is unable to fulfill her duties due to illness, the
responsiblity goes to another woman who has experience in
planning the fiesta. If the *matenadora* dies, then the statue
of the saint under her care is willed to another devoted
follower of the saint who has promised to carry on the
tradition. This person need not be a member of the family
of the deceased *matenadora*.[23]

The position of *matenadora* is a very prestigious one
in the village. Years ago, the statues belonged to *cofradías*,
associations of men and women who were drawn to a
particular image of the saint. These *cofradías* appear to be
African in their traditions. The three distinct images of St.
James the Apostle seems to maintain ancestral groupings
around the categories of age and gender, each with its own
particular function. The statue for the men may correspond
to the fraternity of men who, as devil figures, terrorized and
chased women and children. The statue for the women
appears to be the localized counterpart of a secret society
for women. And the statue for the children may be a
Christian version of an African group dedicated to the
initiation rites for children when they reach puberty.[24]
The more modern *cofradías* were under the direction of a
matenadora. Together the *matenadora* and the *cofradía*
planned the fiesta, raised the funds to pay expenses,
arranged for the *novenas*, and directed the religious

processions. Since the 1950s the *cofradías* have lost their popularity. Now the devotees of a particular image of the saint are those who are obligated to pay the saint back for favors received as well as the family and neighbors of the *matenadora*.[25]

The planning for the fiesta begins each year at the end of June. The *matenadoras* direct the planning meetings which take place in their homes. The funds necessary for the fiesta come from cash donations and raffles of goods donated by local businesses. These funds pay for musicians, the priest to say the masses, paper flowers, and the refreshments served after each evening's *novena*. The necessity for raising money to put on a grand fiesta, as well as the past tradition of the *cofradías*, promotes a rivalry among the *matenadoras*. Each wants the day her image of the saint is at the head of the procession to be the best day of the fiesta. This rivalry has a real economic function. Not only does each *matenadora* solicit donations from local businesses, these same businesses benefit from the trade which the fiesta brings to the village.[26]

Very early in July the women of the village begin making the traditional costumes which the men will wear. There is a relationship between the disguise and the economic status of its wearer. The cost of the costume for the *caballero* is between $300-$500. The *vejigante* costume costs only $60.[27] The other two traditional disguises, that of the *viejo* and the *loca*, are made from everyday clothing. The cost for these two costumes is negligible. This is not to imply that those of higher economic status are necessarily the leaders of the village. Most of the better off Loiceños live elsewhere.

The Schedule of Events

Prior to the fiesta proper, there are nine days of prayer in honor of each of the images of Santiago Apóstol.[28] These *novenas* are generally held in the evening at the homes of the *matenadoras* or guardians of the statues. Each night a statue of Santiago sits on a table in front of the worshippers who, under the direction of the *matenadora*, follow the pattern of the "Novena de Santiago" brought from Spain centuries ago: the rosary, a song to Santiago, a *salve* (prayer for salvation) and another song. This is all done by memory; there are no surviving written texts. A popular *gozo* or hymn to Santiago is:

> We sing, gloriously, to our Patron Santiago, he is a
> man before God, and every soul flies to him. Come,
> come, come here to adore him in faith and love at
> this altar. How brilliantly golden is this happy day
> and all souls fly to him.[29]

The fiesta begins each year very early in the morning. On each July 24 at 4 a.m., a herald runs through the streets of Loíza Aldea announcing the beginning of the traditional fiesta in honor of Santiago Apóstol. Rockets are fired at noon. At 6 p.m. a procession carries the first statue, *Santiago de los hombres* (St. James for the men), from the home where it resides during the year to the pueblo church of San Patricio in the center of the town. An hour later, speeches in the plaza by public officals open the fiesta. Later that night dancing begins in the plaza.

The second day, July 25, is the feast day of Santiago Apóstol. It begins with a mass in the morning at the pueblo church. This day is of particular significance because it is reserved for family reunions and the return of the *ausentes*, those who have been absent during the year. It is also the traditional time when babies are baptized and young people get married. The highlight of the afternoon is the coronation of the queens of the fiesta. In the evening there is an art show in the plaza and dancing.

On July 26, the religious processions for each of the statues of Santiago Apóstol begin. The pattern for each of the three days of processions remains constant. Each statue of the saint has a day, designated by tradition, when it takes the lead at the head of the procession. The other two statues always follow behind it. The statue of *Santiago de los hombres* takes its place as the leader on this day. Early in the afternoon, the statue of *Santiago de los hombres* leaves the pueblo church of San Patricio for the beach known as *Las Carreras* ("the races") in Medianía Alta.[30] It is followed by the statue for the women, *Santiago de las mujeres*, and the statue for the children, *Santiago de los muchachos* or *Santiaguito*. The religious procession is over when the three statues have been returned to the homes of their guardians. In the evening there are masses said in both the pueblo and parish churches. Dancing in the town plaza begins afterwards.

The next day, July 27, is the time when the image of the saint for the women, *Santiago de las mujeres*, takes its place at the front of the processional line. Here, as on the first day, it is followed by the other two images of Santiago Apóstol in the same order as the first day. The art show and evening dancing resume.

The final religious procession for Santiago Apóstol takes place on July 28. On this day *Santiago de los muchachos* is taken to *Las Carreras* first, followed by the image of Santiago for the men and then the women. At 7 p.m. a mass is celebrated in the pueblo church of San Patricio, and the typical evening's entertainment continues.

The 29th of July through the 3rd of August are days of recreation and are thus given over to sporting events, games of chance, eating, drinking, and dancing. The fiesta ends, much as it began, with prayer in the morning and dancing in the evening. Santiago Apóstol makes his public appearance in the religious processions of the fiesta. It is interesting to note that there is no dramatic portrayal of the victory of the Spanish over the Moors as in the Santiago traditions of Spain or Mexico. The focus in Loíza Aldea is on the localized Santiago Apóstol and not on rehearsing the Spanish experience of him. Because this localization of Santiago Apóstol in the home and the street is a major factor in understanding what the saint represents, we will begin to explore the saint's many layers of meaning by discussing the religious processions in detail.

Patterns in the Processions

There is a generic shape to processions. This shape is the movement from place "x" to place "y" in a way that has symbolic significance.[31]   In the fiesta of Santiago Apóstol in Loíza Aldea, this generic shape is structured according to tradition. The route is a simple one. It proceeds down route 187 toward the barrio of Medianía Alta, the fabled area where legend has it that the very first statue of Santiago Apóstol miraculously appeared. The people and an image of the saint move together from one place, the village, to another, the beach (*Las Carreras*), and back to the village.

The order in which the people walk the processional route is included in this basic pattern of movement. At the head of the line are the police. Following them are a jeep with a huge *vejigante* mask mounted on its hood, the flag bearer, each of the three statues carried on a litter by four individuals, the people and the ritual clowns, and a truckload of musicians. Like the route walked, this pattern remains constant.

There is a third pattern in the processions under discussion. The processions are "stational," that is, along the route they stop at predetermined points which have symbolic significance.[32] Each procession leaves the town with a statue of the saint. The procession stops along the way at the cemetery which is just outside of town. Here the dead are honored with a rocket salute. It then proceeds to the homes where the other two statues of the saint are housed. It is at these points that the other two statues enter the processional line. They are greeted at their homes with a flag salute. The flag bearers twirl their flags at each other, and then the statue takes its place in order. When the procession reaches its destination, *Las Carreras*, riders on horseback take the three flags of Santiago Apóstol and ride with them up and down the processional route. The procession ends when all of the statues are returned to their homes.

The high point of the procession is the racing with the red and gold flags of the warrior-saint. These flags are military insignias which have profound symbolic significance. Prior to battle, flags ("the colors") are customarily carried in front of an army to identify it. During battle, flags are used as rallying points for troops. They identify a soldier's group and aid him in regrouping during the chaos of combat. When ground is taken in battle, flags on poles are thrust into the ground as a way of "staking claim" to conquered territory. And finally, when the fighting is over, a flag held high signals victory. In the Middle Ages, *la corrida de las banderas* (running with the flags) was a privilege and a service to the Spanish

Crown.[33] In Loíza Aldea, *la corrida da las banderas* is a
privilege and a service, this time to Santiago Apóstol.

MY EXPERIENCE OF THE PROCESSIONS

It was oven hot that day of the first procession. There
were men drinking beer, casually discarding their empty
bottles along the roadside, and there were women, often
with their hair tied tight in curlers (no doubt in preparation
for the evening's celebrations and dancing), closely
watching children or shading themselves with umbrellas.
Children and youths were everywhere. Some walked,
others jogged, leaving their parents behind in favor of the
company of their friends.

Although the procession clearly dominated the day's
activities, reminders of daily life in Loíza Aldea were
inescapable. There were posters advertising "Winston"
cigarettes and "Don Q" rum. Open-air bars, taverns, and
eateries were jammed with human bodies seeking relief
from the sun with a cold drink. A housing project and a
school, a "cash n' carry" *mercado* (market) and car repair
shop, a beauty parlor and the Ayala art shop dotted the
roadside. The almost middle-class atmosphere of Loíza
Aldea with its bank, Mobil and Shell gasoline stations,
library, pharmacy, police station, civil defense hall, and new
Doña Hilda Restaurant and Cocktail Lounge, could not hide
the poverty along the procession route.

Small wooden, tin-roofed shacks clustered together,
strangely keeping company with the concrete public
housing. Families stood in their doorways. These were not
the *casas* of the *caballeros* who were soon to come on
horseback. These were the homes of people like a lone
caballero who stood outside a bar, riding a "horse"

constructed from a burlap-covered wooden frame. The ease and the liveliness of the procession both concealed and revealed the village's enduring poverty. At the very front of the procession were the motorcycle policemen, riding their mechanized horsepower. They were there ostensibly for traffic control rather than for crowd control. Following the policemen was an open back jeep with the mask it is most known for, the *vejigante,* mounted as a huge hood ornament crafted out of papier-mâché and painted in festive colors. This jeep, as well as the police, and perhaps more so, heralded the arrival of the procession.

A single person followed the jeep. This person had the honor and responsibility of holding high the banner of Santiago Apóstol. The image of the Saint, the center of the procession, came next on a litter supported on the shoulders of four men. Behind the statue were the people. In the rear, was a truck carrying local musicians, horns blaring and drums pounding out *bombas* and *plenas.*[34]

In keeping with the local traditions, the first statue to be carried aloft was that of *Santiago de los hombres.* Four men, chosen by the saint's *matenadora* for their devotion to the saint, walked slowly with a pole across one shoulder, supporting the small white-covered litter upon which the image rested. In front of them a local woman dressed in everyday clothes carried a gold and scarlet banner depicting *Santiago de los hombres.* Its back showed a gold cross mounted on a white crest. The banner read "Viva Santiago Apóstol." The statue itself was a helmeted military figure leaning forward on horseback, sword unsheathed with right arm extended as if ready to charge. Small scallop shells on the statue's helmut and cape recalled the early Christian view of Santiago Apóstol as a simple pilgrim. On the statue's arm were tied several yellow artificial flowers and streaming pink and yellow ribbons. At each corner of the white covered litter were other flowers.

The men and boys dressed as Santiago--the *caballeros*--wore the outfit of a typical Spanish gentleman of the sixteenth century, though noticeably stylized for the festivity of the day. Their faces were hidden by wire-mesh masks with painted red cheeks and black moustache, sometimes enhanced with silver paint which made the masks shine. On their heads the *caballeros* wore satin-covered sombreros with streaming ribbons, colored flowers, and fluffy plumage. Their uniforms were red, green, blue, yellow, black and white, and their capes were covered with small mirrors which reflected the rays of the sun. On their feet were riding boots.

In contrast to the *caballeros* were the *vejigantes*. The *vejigantes* got their name from a noise instrument they once used to scare passersby. Years ago they carried a *vejiga*, or animal bladder, that when pumped like a bellows gave off a whine or shriek. These men were both comic and grotesque in their appearance as they represented the Moors, the devils for an earlier Hispanic Christianity. Wearing the traditional devil masks of Loíza Aldea, they walked or danced down the street.

These masks were carved from dried coconut husks and painted in red, blue, black and white. Their outstanding features included horns that seemed to grow out of their foreheads and a vampire-like grin. Their multi-colored costumes made them look like bats when they raised their arms. Folds of fabric linked wrists to ankles, spreading like wings. They all wore white gloves and kerchiefs hiding any distracting human characteristics.

As they moved down the street, the *vejigantes* hooted, shrieked, and yelled. The quality and quantity of their screams depended only upon their own ingenuity and the elasticity of their voices. Generally missing were the bats and sticks of earlier years used to swat at passersby in a mock attitude of battle.

Teenagers were there in abundance. Among their costumes were high school graduation gowns, gorilla suits, and rubber masks of skulls, monsters, or science fiction characters. The teenagers chased and teased young children, scaring some of the younger ones who clung to their mother's legs, burying their faces deep in their mother's clothing. Costumed children were everywhere. In twos or threes they roamed the streets mimicking the *caballeros* and the *vejigantes* in their appearance and antics. Like their older counterparts, their costumes and masks were fashioned with great care and detail.

These did not exhaust the range of costumed characters in the festival. In keeping with the fiesta's tradition, there were also the *viejos* or old men and the *locas* or "crazy" women. In years past the *viejos* wore simple street clothes and masks cut out of old cardboard shoe boxes. The *viejos* this day wore commercially made rubber masks molded and lined to indicate the wrinkles of age. Under an occasional fedora, large shocks of white hair billowed onto their shoulders.

The *locas*, too, were very contemporary. Although they did not wear a mask years ago, they did paint their faces black. The tradition of face-painting was replaced in this fiesta with make-up. Some *locas* were dressed in stylish wigs, fashionable dresses, heels, and handbags slung over one shoulder. One smoked cigarettes with a long holder. A person might mistake a *loca* for a woman except for one visible difference--the moustache.

The *locas* walked in pairs most of the time, arm in arm like "girlfriends," exchanging jests and jokes with the people as they passed each other along the way. The *locas* were greeted with smiles and laughter. Gone, like the sticks of the *vejigantes*, were the household brooms of earlier days. The *locas* were originally so named because they "swept" the streets wherever they walked and solicited donations from the crowd for their "work".

The procession continued eastward on route 187. Route 187 begins in Isla Verde, a suburb of San Juan, and traces the palm-treed coastline to Loíza Aldea. Before it reaches the village it crosses the *Río Grande de Loíza* (the Great River of Loíza) by means of a hand-pulled ferry, *El Ancón* (the Small Cove). Out of business as of the end of the 1986 fiesta due to the completion of a new bridge, *El Ancón* had been the one link between the banks of Piñones and Loíza Aldea besides small boats dating back to the nineteenth century.[35] On the eastern side of the river, route 187 steps back from the coast and winds its way gradually southward, through farm country, to the town of Río Grande and highway route 3.

After leaving the church of San Patricio in the pueblo, the first of three stations during the procession was the house of the guardian of the statue of *Santiago de los muchachos*. As the procession reached the house of Señora Julia Calcaño, it stopped. Waiting near the road were four women, bearing on their shoulders *Santiaguito*, a small replica of the soldier-saint on horseback, an obvious identification with the size of his followers, the children of Loíza Aldea. Seeming more like a pony than a horse, *Santiaguito's* horse rears back as he holds the reins with one hand, tiny sword upright in the other. Under the front hooves of the horse lies a decapitated head of a Moor. Like *Santiago de los hombres*, his red platform was decorated with flowers, and around its base were tied tiny, silver metal objects fashioned to look like arms, hands, legs, and hearts. These objects represented the ills cured by the saint during the year. A banner held up by a teenage boy greeted the procession of Santiago Apóstol. The images faced each other on the street. On a signal from the leaders who accompanied the statues, each flag bearer and litter saluted the other. The individuals carrying the litters slowly lowered them twice while the flag bearers rolled their banner around in a figure eight design. When the salute was finished, a cheer went up in the crowd, and *Santiaguito* took his place immediately behind the first statue. The same salute was repeated at the second station, the house of the guardian for the image of *Santiago de las mujeres*, Señor Nicolás Pérez Cruz. At first glance, the two larger images of Santiago looked alike. But there are subtle differences that helped distinguish them. Unlike *Santiago de los hombres*, *Santiago de las mujeres* holds his sword in a more upright position; his right wrist was tied with a couple of pink and yellow ribbons. His white cape lies against his back, not catching the breeze like *Santiago de los hombres*, as he looks, almost gently to one side.

Three miles down route 187, past the parish church of Santiago Apóstol, the procession turned onto route 965 to *Las Carreras* and the sea. As the procession approached the turn-off, the *caballeros*, the men dressed as Santiago himself, waited on horseback in a small clearing to the left. Gradually they joined the procession at the rear. When we reached *Las Carreras*, the races, each would be invited to take a banner from one of the three figures and gallop down the street, banner flapping in the breeze, in a symbolic reminder of *Santiago Matamoros*, Saint James, Vanquisher of the Moors, Patron Saint of Spain, Defender of Puerto Rico's military during the Spanish colonial empire, and adopted Saint, the Benefactor of Loíza Aldea. The heat of the day, the red and gold, the sounds of the *bomba*, the encircling smells of beer, perfume, and manure, the setting off of firecrackers and rockets, all combined in a charge upon the senses.

The second day was the day for *Santiago de las mujeres*. This time I decided to take a different perspective on the fiesta. I decided not to walk in the procession but to drive to the church of Santiago Apóstol in Medianía Alta. When I returned to Loíza Aldea on the second day, I became locked in a line of cars that took nearly an hour of bumper-to-bumper edging forward to travel the route up to the church of Santiago Apóstol. As the line of cars I was in approached the church on the corner, everything was at a standstill. The people had blocked the road at the intersection of routes 187 and 965. They were dancing the *bomba* in the street. The band in the truck was parked directly in front of the church with a crowd of people beside it. People were everywhere. They were even on the roof of the church. I thought that I was locked in Loíza forever. People on foot, motorcycles, bicycles, and horses made manuvering difficult, if not impossible. Some people simply got out of their cars and joined in the dancing. Eventually the caravan I was in began to move. When each car reached the glut of people in front of the church, it was greeted by the loud afro-antillean strains of the *bomba* and a daring *vejigante* who danced oh so suavely within the inches allowed him between cars. I remembered this *vejigante* from the first day because of his dazzling costume and traditional Ayala mask. I applauded him, to the pleasure of his audience, as I waited to move. Finally loose from the crowd, I crept forward.

This car trip to Medianía Alta offered me another perspective on the fiesta. The *viejos* and *locas* seemed to be everywhere. One *viejo* rode a horse and wore, in addition to his costume, a long, black stove-pipe hat. The *locas*, the young men dressed as women, did not adopt the exaggerated derrieres and bustlines that, with their brooms, were once their trademark. This time they mimicked the clothing and mannerisms of Puerto Rican women. Wearing make-up and necklaces, carrying purses, wigs meticulously coiffed, these elegantly dressed young "women" walked along teasing each other and the townspeople. Only a few children, of ambiguous gender, wore the more traditional *loca* black paint, kerchief tied around the head, and modest clothing.

On the third day of the processions *Santiaguito* is honored with the same celebrations. These three days, July 26-28, are the core of the fiesta of Santiago Apóstol, the days when the images of the saint are brought into public view.

July 25th, the feast day of Santiago Apóstol, is also Constitution Day in Puerto Rico, a national holiday commemorating the establishment of Puerto Rico as a "free associated state" of the United States. It is also the day when the *Independentistas* rally at the port of Gúanica on the southwest coast of Puerto Rico to protest Puerto Rico's dependent territorial status. They do so at Gúanica because this was the July 25th landing site for the invasion by the United States Marines in 1898. In that year Puerto Rico was ceded to the United States by Spain according to the terms of the Treaty of Paris which ended the Spanish-American War. July 28th is another national holiday. It honors the memory of Señor José Celso Barbosa, one of the original proponents of Statehood for Puerto Rico which, not so incidentally, is the political choice for the majority of Loiceños.

CHANGING PLACES

The work of Victor W. Turner is particularly helpful in understanding the religious processions in the fiesta of Santiago Apóstol as ritual processes or condensations of a larger social process. Turner describes both the ritual and social processes as passages from structure to anti-structure to structure.[37] Structure is his term for the social arrangements which separate people by defining their differences in terms of status, roles, and hierarchies. The institutionalization of these social arrangements demonstrates the enduring reality of structure.[38]

These institutionalized social arrangements are, however, only one half of social life. The ritual process, as a condensation of the process of social life, displays the totality of social life as a dialogue between structure and anti-structure, between fixed states and the transitional periods between those fixed states.[39] The transition phase Turner calls "liminality." Liminality arises out of the necessary interstices within structure. These intervals, in turn, make structure possible. Without them there would be no possibility for construing the differences which constitute structure.[40]

The other side of liminality is that it provides the ground for the temporary ritual suspension of differences among people.[41] This temporary suspension generates a sense of "communitas," that is, "undifferentiated, equalitarian, direct, extant, nonrational, existential relationships" which are "spontaneous, immediate, concrete."[42] The relationships which emerge out of communitas ignore, reverse, or cut across the fixed states so characteristic of structure.[43]

The passage from structure to anti-structure to structure mirrors the process in the rites of passage studied by Arnold Van Gennep. In *The Rites of Passage*, Van Gennep describes the three phases which Turner adapted for his understanding of social and ritual processes. These three phases are separation, transition, and reincorporation. In the ritual process, the separation phase is one which symbolically detaches the ritual subject (Turner's term) from its place in the social structure.[44] The transition phase is the liminal, or threshold, period. It is in this phase that the place of the ritual subject in the social structure becomes decidedly ambiguous, because the ritual subject can no longer be identified according to social conventions.[45] The phase of reincorporation is the end of the passage. Reincorporation returns the ritual subject to a stable place within the social structure. Once again the norms and values of the social structure are incumbent upon the ritual subject.[46]

This process, or passage, usually takes one of two ritual forms: status elevation or status reversal. In a status elevation ritual, the ritual subject is translated from a lower state to a higher one in the social structure with its attendant rights and obligations.[47] This change in positions is irreversible. Examples of status elevation rituals are those which pertain to life crises, namely, birth, puberty, marriage, and death. They are rituals which cannot be repeated.

A status reversal ritual is customarily tied to a calender, is repeatable, and transitory. A ritual subject of low status is translated to a higher status in this ritual. Accompanying this change of status is the temporary exercise of previously unknown authority over one's superior who, due to his or her reciprocal status reversal, must endure ridicule and shame at the hands of the "new" superior.[48]

Whereas rituals of status elevation mark crucial transitional states in a social structure which mirror the life cycle, rituals of status reversal display the fundamental and fixed social categories of the ritual subject.[49]   As such, the social categories are reaffirmed as unchanging. However, Turner points out that both ritual forms, status elevation and status reversal, reflect and reinforce the social structure. In the end, the system of social relations goes unchallenged.[50]

STATUS REVERSAL AS SYMBOLIC DISLOCATION

The religious processions in the fiesta of Santiago Apóstol are rituals of status reversal. These status reversals take the form of symbolic dislocations in some of the customary patterns in the village's social life. Symbolic dislocation is a helpful nuance on Turner's concept of liminality. A concept provided by Roberto DaMatta, symbolic dislocation is the movement of an element from one domain to another where it does not normally belong. This transition makes the element stand out in a way that it never would if it never moved. Because it stands out, the element becomes the locus where relationships which are basic to a group find themselves inverted or exaggerated, and, the differences are, for a time, neutralized.[51]   This concept of symbolic dislocation is not the same as Mary Douglas's concept of misplacement or "matter out of place."   Since it does not spoil patterns but only exaggerates them, symbolic dislocation is not threatening like misplacement.   Symbolic dislocation preserves structure, not by rejecting the incongruous, that is, anti-structure, but by repeating the incongruity and thereby, focusing on it. This incongruity, then, becomes a reference point for viewing structure in a new way.

The symbolic dislocations in the religious processions of Santiago Apóstol give us clues to the meaning of the processions. A close examination of the religious processions reveals three highly suggestive symbolic dislocations. Each of the three religious processions is a movement which conveys an image of the saint from a home into the street. This change of place is significant because statues of saints are traditionally tied to a cathedral or shrine and not a parishoner's home. When in the street, each image moves from the village plaza to the seashore and then back to its home. This circular route is important because it retraces, in reverse order, the passage of the original statue from the beach to the church in the plaza and back. The original statue was an image of *Santiaguito*. This identification is provocative because in the fiesta for Santiago Apóstol in Loíza Aldea there are three statues of the saint, one each for the men, the women, and the children. Said to be the most miraculous of all the images of the saint, *Santiaguito* is not recognized by the Roman Catholic Church. This discrepancy between popular piety and official Church legislation is further emphasized by the fact that the Church teaches that only one statue of a saint is acceptable for the devotion of the people.[52] This one image is *Santiago de los hombres*.[53] The continued veneration of all three statues, in violation of Church law, offers us, along with the other two symbolic dislocations, leading clues regarding the meaning of the religious processions.

The recognition of only one image of the saint by the church over against the practice of the people presents us with an interesting dynamic in the fiesta. As we will see in the next chapter, the masked figures in the fiesta are instrumental symbols. This means that without them the meaning of the dominant symbol, St. James the Apostle, represented in the statues would remain clouded. The same is true for the internal structure of the statues themselves. If the fiesta celebrated its patron saint with only one statue, the fiesta would have a very different face. The question remains, however, which statue among the three is dominant and which statues are instrumental? There are two answers to this question depending upon which side of religion one is on. If one sides with the official religion of the Church, then clearly, *Santiago de los hombres* is dominant. If, however, one sides with the popular practice of the people, then without a doubt, the state of *Santiaguito* is dominant. This perspective makes the statues for the men and for the women instrumental for the people whereas for the Church the statues for the women and the children "technically" do not exist as they are not officially recognized. For the Church maleness is preeminent whereas for the people life is better characterized, perhaps, as a transition from childhood to adulthood.

With these clues, we can examine what the processions have to say. One conclusion is that the transition from high to low is crucial for understanding the religious processions.[53] Santiago Apóstol displays many of the characteristics associated with a ritual subject who is in the liminal phase of a ritual process.[54] He is compassionate, affectionate, humble, equalitarian, and of low rank. In an almost creedal statement by Loiceño serigraph artist Samuel Lind, the popular beliefs of the people of Loíza Aldea regarding the saint are described:

> Santiago Matamoros, Lord of war and storms,
> guardian of the fishermen, the sugar cane cutters, and
> the coconut farmers, is harsh with the wicked, the

protector of the poor, kind to women, and affectionate with children. He is a humble Santiago who came here to Loíza, drank water from the fruit of the palm trees, and remained forever, rejoicing and suffering with us.[55]

These liminal characteristics are reflected and reinforced in the three images of the saint carried in the religious processions. The saint begins with a lowly status because he lives in a home during the year. When he enters the street, and is carried aloft on a litter, he is elevated. As we will see later, this elevation is really an elevation of the people of Loíza Aldea, who, like Santiago Apóstol, endure a low status during the rest of the year.

The saint's low status is also reiterated by his processional route. It takes him back to the sea and not to the plaza church. Because not all of the three images of the saint are recognized by the Church, the saint cannot take up residence in the church. The statues of the saint which represent the women and the children in the village, by being unacceptable to the Church, reiterate the unacceptibility of treating women and children as equal to men. But for the people, the most miraculous statue resembles a child. This, in turn, makes Santiago Apóstol in the view of the people symbolize the most powerless segments of the village.

We see in the images of Santiago Apóstol a transition from the legendary patron saint of Spain, the warrior-saint, to a localized Santiago Apóstol who lives, rejoices, and suffers with the people of Loíza Aldea. This Santiago Apóstol bears a resemblance to the saint of legend, but in his passage from structure to anti-structure to structure, the Santiago Apóstol of Loíza Aldea has reversed the passage of the original legendary sky spirit. Unlike the

patron saint of Spain who descended from the heavens only
to return, the patron saint of Loíza Aldea has remained with
the people. His passage in the religious processions is a
movement from lowliness to high stature to lowliness, like
the people he represents. This symbolic dislocation of the
original myth of Santiago Apóstol has something to say
about the people's religious convictions, local history,
ethnic identity, and social relationships.

Religious Convictions

The religious convictions of the people of Loíza
Aldea, although focused on Santiago Apóstol as benefactor
and protector, comment upon the larger oppositions of the
sacred and the profane as well. In the religious
processions, the sacred and profane spheres of life are
inverted. Rather than taking place in a church sanctuary
and being led by priests, the religious processions take
place in the streets and are led by the villagers. The street,
the place of commerce, travel, and the secular life, becomes
a sacred path. The street becomes sacred because of what
happens there: the coming together of Santiago Apóstol
and his people. In the religious processions, Santiago and
the people take their worship out of the church building, out
of the control of the priests, and bring it into the streets.
Their religious processions, then, are liturgies of the streets,
public services to the sacred, without walls. Because they
are without walls, these liturgies are open to the intrusion
of chaos. We will see this more clearly when we discuss
the ritual clowns who, as images of chaos, are not welcome
inside the church building.

In keeping with the Church's general disdain for the
religious processions as "pagan" rites,[57] the Church plays

a minimal role in the festivities. The fiesta includes several masses, but the local priest takes no part in the religious processions or the *novenas* which are held in honor of Santiago Apóstol just prior to the opening of the fiesta. These liturgies of the streets bear a resemblance to the mass[57] in its actions[58] of taking, blessing, breaking, and remembering.

During the religious processions there is a taking, or offering, made to Santiago Apóstol. These offerings are the acts of hospitality which the people of Loíza Aldea exchange with each other in honor of the saint who presides over the fiesta. In the village's welcoming of visitors, these offerings can also be seen. The people's homes reverse their daily privacy and open themselves up to the public, offering refreshment to family and strangers alike. Sharing a meal, or part of one, is universally recognized as an intimate or familial gesture.

In the religious processions the blessing takes the form of men and women carrying the images of Santiago Apóstol on litters, the gifts of ribbons that adorn the images, the flowers that ornament the litters, and the silver arms, legs, hands, and feet that surround the figure of *Santiaguito* at its base. This obligatory act of paying back the saint for his help is eucharistic in that it is a giving thanks to the saint for his assistance with troubles or illnesses during the year.

The breaking is the sacrifice of the self in service to the saint. The simple walking of the procession route behind the saint is the form of this action.[59] The action of remembering is not only recalling the great deeds of the saint publically and privately. It is re-membering, reconstituting the oneness of the village with its saint. This re-membering takes the form of the religious processions as a whole.

Local History

The village's local history is also condensed in Santiago Apóstol. In his high position as the legendary warrior sky spirit, Santiago Apóstol was the quintessential Spanish conqueror, the slayer of the enemies of Spain. As conqueror, he was also the master, the oppressor. In his low status in Loíza Aldea, Santiago dislocates himself from this image and myth and identifies himself with the Loiceños and their history of conquest, slavery, and colonization. Santiago no longer takes the part of the conqueror, he is the conquered. Santiago is no longer the overseer, he is the slave. Santiago is not a colonizer, he is a Puerto Rican. In his identification with the people, the saint abolishes all the class distinctions which, as the *Matamoros,* put him above the people. He also minimizes the role of the Catholic priest in the fiesta as he claims this role for himself by presiding over the religious processions.[60] With another oppressor put in his place, Santiago Apóstol demonstrates again that he belongs to the people. He is a child the people. He is their servant.[61]

Ethnic Identity

The white-skinned faces of the images of Santiago Apóstol can easily be misunderstood. As the patron saint of a former slave community, one might ask why the faces of the saint are not painted black. The faces of the saint are not painted black because Santiago Apóstol represents the ideal of the Spanish upper classes in Puerto Rico. It must be noted the first fiestas for Santiago Apóstol took place in San Juan in the early years of the conquest.[62]

And, although since then, Puerto Rican society has absorbed people of color, blacks generally still occupy the lowest rung of the social ladder.[63] In this localized Santiago Apóstol, the patron saint of Spain is re-membered. In the three statues of Santiago Apóstol, the mixture of Spanish, Taíno Indian, and African blood in Puerto Ricans is recognized only in that the white faces of the statues deny it. As we discussed in chapter two, the status that accompanies being white in Puerto Rican society is deeply rooted in the island's history. Historically, whiteness is associated with power that comes from the wealth and education which the Spaniards brought to the New World. As we will see in the next chapter, the masks of the ritual clowns reiterate this message. The clown which represents the saint has a white face. The saint's masked counterpart, the devil, is not only likened to Yoruba sculpture by Ricardo E. Alegría,[64] its appearance suggests a caricature of the African with its customarily dark face, oversized nose, and thick lips. The masks, other than that for the saint, portray the typical groups associated with being non-white. Today these groups are people of color, the poor, and females. Yesterday they were the slaves, the laborers, and, not surprisingly, females.

Social Relationships

The Spanish legend of Santiago Apóstol put the saint, as we have seen before, in a high position as the *Matamoros*. This former Spanish slayer of Moors and African warrior sky spirit becomes, in his low status in Loíza Aldea, Santiago the life-giver. He still is the benefactor of the people, but his mode of operation has changed. He is the companion of the people, the one who

remains with them, affectionate and kind. The tone set by
Santiago Apóstol in Loíza Aldea tells us something about
the social relationships within the village. His three images
are very informative in this regard. These three images
recapitulate each of the main components of the village,
and, in so doing, level the social statuses based upon
gender, age, and residence. The social differences
determined by gender are collapsed in the image of
Santiago de las mujeres. Along with the other two images,
the members of the ideal Puerto Rican family, father,
mother, and child, are represented as equals, contradicting
the Church's positioning of the male-father as the head of
the household with his accompanying rights and privileges.
In addition, the legend of the original statue, that of
Santiaguito, in its exaggeration, is an indication of the
premium put on children within the family, and by
extension, the family within the community. The
prominence of the family in the village is also suggested by
the tradition that the fiesta is a time for the baptism of
children and courting among the youth of the village.
Children are also full participants in the fiesta. They not
only have their own statue of the saint, boys dress up as
caballeros and *vejigantes,* and little girls are chosen as
queens of the fiesta. It is not just the immediate family that
is intended. As the statues of Santiago Apóstol
symbolically represent father, mother, and children, they
also include, by extension, the pueblo.[65]

The community, in turn, extends beyond its
geographical boundaries. Those who live in Loíza Aldea
year-round are not the only ones to participate in the
celebration for Santiago Apóstol. The saint embraces all
the Loiceños who have been absent during the year, the
ausentes. He also honors the dead. The *ausentes* are
remembered during a time that is set aside for a reunion at

the beginning of the fiesta. The dead are remembered with a salute at the cemetery just after each religious procession begins. In the fiesta, the whole family of Loíza Aldea is acknowledged. The fiesta is more than a tourist attraction promoted by the government; it is an intimate family reunion. It is the community's retelling of its family history and traditions by walking through them. The religious processions from the plaza, through the barrios, and to the coast, are a rehearsal of a common past. The processional route from the plaza, Spain's contribution to the New World's urban design and community life,[66] built upon the same ground where there once stood a *yucayeque,* links the plaza to the coast, where the Taíno Indians fished, and the place where slaves fought alongside their masters in order to protect the island from invaders. The processional route is a loop which extends from the center of the village, to the sea, and back to the village. Within its boundaries it encompasses the whole family of Loíza Aldea and its shared history.

CONCLUSION

This is not all there is to the story. So far we have discussed what the saint, imaged as three in one, has to say. There is another side to this story. We have looked at the dissolution of differences which is characteristic of *communitas. Communitas,* however, not only holds up to view the best possible world, it also holds a spotlight on the darker, private areas of village life. To these areas, we must now turn our attention.

In keeping with lived experience, the religious processions as ritual processes show both sides of life: what can be and what is. Up to this point we have discussed the benefits of *communitas*, its leveling of oppositions. It is the same *communitas*, however, which, while it points to the abolition of differences, reminds us of those very same differences. Thus, while the images of the saint and the trek to the beach tell one story, there is another story contained within the same symbolic dislocations. Now it is time to look at how the fuller picture is portrayed in the ritual clowns, how they reveal what is concealed through their masks and disguises.

NOTES

1. "The law of prayer is the law of belief" refers to the authority of liturgy and liturgical practice. Originally an axiom of Prosper of Aquitane, and later attributed to Pope Celestine I, "lex orandi, lex credendi" may also be understood as "the rule of prayer should lay down the rule of faith." See Jaroslav Pelikan, *The Christian Tradition: A History of the Development of Doctrine*, vol. 3, *The Growth of Medieval Theology (600-1300)* (Chicago: The University of Chicago Press, 1978), 67.

2. The Spanish word *fiesta* comes from the Latin term for *festival*, that is, *festum* or "public joy, merriment, revelry." However, as Alessandro Falassi points out, there were two terms in Latin for festival, the other being *feria* or "absence from work in honor of the gods." Falassi also notes that *festum* and *feria* were used in the plural, *festa* and *feriae* respectively, demonstrating that festivals lasted for several days and included many events. See Alessandro Falassi, "Festival: Definition and Morphology," in *Time Out of Time: Essays on the Festival*, ed. Alessandro Falassi (Albuquerque: University of New Mexico Press, 1967), 1-2.

3. Robert Anthony Orsi in his book, *The Madonna of 115th Street: Faith and Community in Italian Harlem, 1880-1950* (New Haven: Yale University Press, 1985), makes a similiar point on page 133.

4. Don Handelman, "The Ritual Clown: Attributes and Affinities," *Anthropos* 76 (1981): 342.

5. *Communitas* is Victor W. Turner's term for the temporary experience of spontaneous communion among people which can happen in liminal situations.

6. *The New Westminster Dictionary of Liturgy and Worship*, ed. J.G. Davies (Philadelphia: The Westminster Press, 1986), 474.

7. *The Study of Liturgy*, eds. Cheslyn Jones, Geoffrey Wainwright, Edward Yarnold, S.J. (New York: Oxford University Press, 1978), 424.

8. See David L. Ungerlieder Kepler, *Fiestas Afro-Borincanas y Cambio Social en Puerto Rico: El Caso de Loíza*, (Mexico: Escuela Nacional de Anthropologia e Historia, M.A. Thesis, 1983), 102-104. The reference to Shangó is significant because Puerto Rican scholars attribute the greatest African influence on the village to be from the Yorubas. See also Ricardo E. Alegría, *La Fiesta de Santiago Apóstol en Loíza Aldea*, 22.

9. St. James the Apostle refers to St. James the Great who is so named to distinguish him from St. James the Less. The New Testament identifies St. James the Great as a son of Zebedee and the brother of St. John (Matt. 4:21). He witnessed the Transfiguration (Matt. 17:1-3) and the Agony in the Garden (Matt. 26:36-38).

10. The Moorish occupation of Spain lasted from the 8th to the 15th century.

11. T.D. Kendrick, *St. James in Spain* (London: Methuen and Co., Ltd., 1960), 18-19.

12. *Ibid.*, 22-23.

13. The municipality of Loíza has several *barrios* or neighborhoods, two of which are Medianía Baja and Medianía Alta.

14. This date is given by Don Castor Ayala in an interview with Henrietta Yurchenco. The interview is recorded in her book *¡Hablamos!* *Puerto Ricans Speak* (New York: Praeger Publishers, 1971), 50.

15. Ricardo E. Alegría recounts for us the traditions regarding the first statue of St. James the Apostle in his book, *La Fiesta de Santiago Apóstol en Loíza Aldea* (San Juan, Puerto Rico: Colección de Estudios Puertorriqueños, 1954), 23-25. The following translation is mine.

Concerning the origin of the images of the Saint which are used in the fiesta, the oral tradition of the town conserves interesting narratives. Though the recognized versions differ, all coincide in that one of the images, the St. James of the children, or Santiaguito, as it is popularly called, appeared miraculously many years ago. There exists, nevertheless, some discrepancy about the way it was discovered. One of the more popular variations relates that many years ago a little old woman was bathing on the beach at Medianía Alta, on the site which today is known as "Las Carreras" (the races); she saw the image of the Saint which came in on a wave. On two occasions the little old woman tried to take it, but always the wave receded, carrying with it the image. The priest of the town was notified, who rushed to the place and, after "offering a prayer," miraculously succeeded in taking the image in his hands. The Saint was carried to the church where it was deposited. On the morning of the next day, he discovered that, during the night, the image had returned to the site where it had been found. One time more the Saint was carried to the church after it had again returned to the beach. Befitting this miracle, the image was sent to Rome, where a reproduction was made which was sent to Loíza, and it is that which is known today as the St. James of the Children.

Another version tells that a man named Atilano Villanueva, who was plowing with oxen on the farm of Doña Juana Lanzó and José Maria Villanueva, in Medianía Alta, found an image under a cork tree that was near the beach. Atilano took the image and carried it to the church, but that night the Saint returned to the site where it had been found. For a second time the Saint returned to the tree. Insisting that this was a miracle, Doña Juana Lanzó gave her lands at the particular site for celebrating the fiesta of the Saint, and since then, every year for St. James, the Saints are carried to this place, today known as "Las

Carreras," because it is here where various horseriders receive the honor of running with the flags of the Saints.

16. Louise L. Cripps, *The Spanish Caribbean: From Columbus to Castro* (Boston, Mass.: G.K. Hall and Co., 1979), 58.

17. Alegría, 22-23. Although Alegría makes this point, this does not mean that there still is any conscious association between these two African spirits and Santiago Apóstol. Rather, any conscious association would be more in keeping with *la religion negra,* the black religion of the area which is comparable to Santería.

18. Robert Farris Thompson, *Flash of the Spirit: African and Afro-American Art and Philosophy* (New York: Random House, 1983), 85.

19. *Ibid.*

20. E. Bolaji Idowu, *Olódùmarè: God in Yoruba Belief* (New York: Frederick A. Praeger, Publishers, 1963), 85.

21. Thompson, 52. It should also be noted that Shangó and Ogun are often conflated with St. Barbara in the Spanish-speaking Caribbean. St. Barbara, with her allusions to thunder, lightning, fire, and iron, was the patron of the artillery men of the fort, *El Morro,* which still stands in Old San Juan.

22. A fiesta may be defined as "any event marking the ritual observance of particular occasions which has as its features an organized personnel, a systematic and traditional structure and content, and a complex of ritual obligations. Eating and the drinking of alcoholic beverages are always part of a fiesta, while music and dancing are often included .... It is not restricted to a single kind of event; but at the same time, it does not take place on *any* occasion; those events which are marked by a fiesta can be clearly enumerated. Further, any fiesta has a ritual character, in the sense that the fiesta and the event it marks are clearly, systematically, and inseparably associated, and that supernatural aid is expected as a result of the performance of prescribed behavior patterns." William Mangin, *The Cultural Significance of the Fiesta Complex in an*

Indian Hacienda in Peru (Yale University: Ph.D. Dissertation, 1954), I-1, quoted in Smith, 5.

23. Alegría, 28.

24. These allusions to African traditions are made by Fernando Ortiz in his prologue to Alegría, xviii.

25. *Ibid.*

26. *Ibid.*, 29.

27. Pastora Carrasquillo, wife of Don Castor Ayala, personal communication.

28. These days of prayer are not part of the fiesta which officially begins on July 24.

29. Alegría, 73.

30. This is the tradition. In recent years, the statue leaves from the plaza and not the church.

31. Barabara Kirshenblatt-Gimblett and Brooks McNamara, "Processional Performance: An Introduction," *Drama Review* 29 (Fall 1985): 2.

32. In his study of late antique and early medieval stational (mobile) liturgies, John F. Baldovin defines the essential characteristics of such liturgies this way: "Stational liturgy is a service of worship at a designated church, shrine, or public place in or near a city or town, on a designated feast, fast, or commemoration, which is presided over by the bishop or his representative and intended as the local church's main liturgical celebration of the day." Baldovin is careful to point out that stational liturgies should not be identified with eucharistic celebrations exclusively. His definition is helpful for this study even with its emphasis on episcopal participation, participation which is antithetical to the popular celebration of the village. See John F. Baldovin, S.J., *The Urban Character of Christian Worship: The Origins, Development, and*

Meaning of Stational Liturgy, Orientalia Christiana Analecta, ed. Robert F. Taft, S.J., no. 228 (Roma: Pont. Institutum Studiorum Orientalium, 1987), 36-37. See also note 6.

33. *Las Fiestas de Santiago Apóstol en Loíza*, produced by Ramón H. Almodóvar and Jaime Hamilton Márquez and directed by Luis Martínez Sosa, 57 min., Producciones Vejigante, Inc. and La Fundación de las Humanidades Puertorriqueñas, 1982. Videocassette.

34. *Bombas* and *plenas* signify both the music and the dances themselves. Specifically, *bombas* come from the sugar plantations of the seventeenth century. A mixture of the Indian, Spanish, and African cultures of Puerto Rico, the *bomba* "depends on an ensemble of two or three drums. The focal point of the dance is a sort of contest between the leading drummer and a particular dancer. The dancer challenges the drummer by improvising steps that the latter must try to match on his instrument. If the drummer is unable to follow the steps, he loses; if the dancer runs out of improvisations, he or she loses." Quoted from Kenneth M. Bilby, "The Caribbean as a Musical Region," in *Carribean Contours*, eds. Sidney W. Mintz and Sally Price, (Baltimore: The Johns Hopkins University Press, 1985), 191. It should also be noted that male dancers compete with their feet and female dancers with their skirts. The *plena* dates back to the nineteenth century. Characteristically, it describes a popular event.

35. In 1988, *El Ancón* was again operating, carrying passengers only, instead of cars.

36. Victor W. Turner, *Dramas, Fields, and Metaphors: Symbolic Action in Human Society* (Ithaca, New York: Cornell University Press, 1974), 282.

37. Victor W. Turner, *The Ritual Process: Structure and Anti-Structure* (Ithaca, New York: Cornell University Press, 1969), 126, 166. See also *Dramas, Fields, and Metaphors*, 274.

38. Turner, *The Ritual Process*, 97, 127.

39. *Ibid.*, 201.

40. Turner, *Dramas, Fields, and Metaphors*, 288.

41. *Ibid.*, 274.

42. *Ibid.*

43. Turner, *The Ritual Process*, 94.

44. *Ibid.*

45. *Ibid.*, 95.

46. *Ibid.*, 167.

47. *Ibid.*

48. *Ibid.*, 176.

49. *Ibid.*, 201.

50. Roberto DaMatta, "Carnival in Multiple Planes," in *Rite, Drama, Festival, Spectacle: Rehearsals Toward a Theory of Cultural Performance*, Ed. John J. MacAloon (Philadelphia: Institute for the Study of Human Issues, Inc., 1984), 213-214.

51. See the 1969 *General Instruction on the Liturgy*, Sec. XI: "Images for Veneration by the Faithful," par. 278 in *The Liturgy Documents: A Parish Resource*, ed. Gabe Huck (Chicago: Liturgy Training Program, The Archdiocese of Chicago, 1980).

52. Ungerlieder Kepler, 104.

53. Turner, *The Ritual Process*, 97.

54. *Ibid.*, 95-96.

55. This description of Santiago Apóstol is part of Samuel Lind's serigraph entitled "Fiestas 87." The translation is mine.

56. Ungerlieder Kepler, 107.

57. Without a priest presiding at the service, the service cannot be construed as a mass or eucharist, that is, the offering of the body and blood of Christ to God on behalf of the people.

58. These actions mirror the four-fold action of Christ at the Last Supper recounted in the institution narrative of St. Paul. See I Corinthians 11:23-24, that is, "... the Lord Jesus on the night when he was betrayed *took* bread, and when he had *given thanks*, he *broke* it, and said, "This is my body which is for you. Do this *in remembrance* of me." Emphasis mine.

59. DaMatta, 218.

60. With the liturgical renewal of the Roman Catholic Church following Vatican II came a change in terminology regarding the role of the priest in the liturgy (mass). A priest no longer "says" mass, nor does he "celebrate" it. He presides over the rite.

61. The Greek term *pais*, used for example in the early church liturgy *The Apostolic Tradition of Hippolytus* to address Christ, makes this connection between child and servant. It is not unlike the use of the term "boy" in some parts of the United States. Though "boy" is used in a derogatory sense to mean both child and servant, the principle is the same.

62. *Las Fiestas de Santiago Apóstol en Loíza*. Videocassette.

63. Hendrik Hoetink, *Caribbean Race Relations: A Study of Two Variants*, trans. Eva M. Hooykaas (London: Oxford University Press, 1967), 39-40.

64. Alegría, 22.

65. The term "pueblo" refers not only to the town but to its inhabitants as well.

66. George McClelland Foster, *Culture and Conquest: America's Spanish Heritage* (Chicago: Quadrangle Books, 1960), 34,48.

4

THE RITUAL CLOWNS

INTRODUCTION

Masking is virtually a universal phenomenon. This "second face" transforms the face for symbolic purposes.[1] The mask conceals the wearer and reveals another. This other is often a mysterious or supernatural being. The various meanings of the term "mask" indicate this. The Spanish word for mask, *máscara*, has entered into our own English vocabulary. For us it denotes a cosmetic preparation used to darken eyelashes. In Spanish, *máscara* connotes "many faces" where before there was only one. The Arabic word, *maskharah*, from which the Spanish word is derived, is particularly apt for this discussion of the masked figures in the fiesta of Santiago Apóstol. *Maskharah* means "buffoon."[2] In this chapter, the term "mask" covers both the comic and the supernatural.

The masked figures in the fiesta not only wear masks, they are masks. They are veils. They conceal the wearer's face while revealing the hidden face of another. These two levels in masking coincide in a ritual context. Ronald L. Grimes describes how a mask works as a symbol of supernatural or mysterious power.[3] A mask concretizes the power in one place, the masked figure. The masked figure simultaneously conceals the power while making it transparent. Raw power is not expressed in the masked

99

figure. It is embodied power, that is, the appearance of power. In the fiesta of Santiago Apóstol, this embodied power takes the form of a challenge to the norms and values of the social order while it upholds those very same structures.

It is important to add that the masks worn in the fiesta are not sacred objects. They are openly sold to tourists. These masks also do not effect any obvious change in the person who wears one. The observer always knows that the masked figures are fully human. Children may be frightened by the masked figures but this is not out of the ordinary. Little else can be said about the transformation, if any, that takes place within the one who wears one of the fiesta's masks. This study is not a pyschological treatment of identity formation nor integration within the individual. It is oriented to the social context.

Called *las máscaras* (the masks) by Loiceños, these masked figures resist simple explanation. At first glance their meaning seems easy enough to grasp. The *caballero* after all is St. James, and the *vejigante* is the devil. But, we are stopped in our tracks with the *viejo* and the *loca*. An old man paired with a crazy woman makes no sense at all. The problem then is to find an interpretive tool which makes intelligible all four masked figures. We know that they relate to each other in some way. They are the traditional masked figures of Loíza Aldea's fiesta, and they are all portrayed by men.

The interpretive tool lies not with the masks themselves. They are merely clues. The real detective work begins when we see that the four masked figures can be seen as ritual clowns. The term "ritual clown" is a technical one. Although it has been defined in several ways, most of the definitions fall into psychological or sociological categories. On the psychological side there are

four basic definitions: 1) a ritual clown reduces the tension
and anxiety generated by the sacred coming in contact with
human beings. Through a rather "harmless burlesque" of
the sacred, the sacred becomes familiar and nonthreatening;
2) a ritual clown concretizes psychological tensions,
especially sexual aggressivness, by bringing those tensions
up to the level of conscious thought; 3) a ritual clown
breaks social and religious taboos by acting them out, thus
diminishing public guilt and anxiety about the taboos; and
4) a ritual clown aids in the public acceptance and
heightened awareness of commonly accepted aspects of a
social order.[4]

The sociological side also offers four basic
definitions: 1) a ritual clown reinforces cultural interests by
highlighting important values and conflicts; 2) social
tensions are reduced by a ritual clown as it aids in the
public identification with traditions through its portrayal of
those traditions; 3) a ritual clown, as an agent of the sacred,
serves as a supernatural sanction to the social order; and 4)
socialization and enculturation are fostered by a ritual
clown as it brings out into the open the salient
characteristics of the social order.[5]

My understanding of ritual clowns is closest to that
of Don Handelman who defines a ritual clown as

> an ambivalent figure of danger and enticement,
> gravity and hilarity, solemnity and fun--[who] appears
> within a frame of messages about the sacredness, the
> truth, and the authenticity of experience. This matrix
> of contrasting (and clashing) attributes is crucial to
> the appreciation of the affinities between the ritual-
> clown and the ideas of 'process' and of
> 'boundariness,' on the one hand, and the affinities
> between deity-figures and ideas of 'anti-structure,' on
> the other.[6]

Handelman picks up the common understanding of ritual clowns as ambiguous figures. His contribution to the discussion is that he sees ritual clowns not only as ambiguous figures in ritual but also as ambiguous figures in and of themselves. Their internal ambiguity points to the ambiguity characteristic of the rituals in which they appear.[7] The fiesta of Santiago Apóstol is no exception. Ritual clowns are known by several names: fool, clown, idiot, jester, wild man, trickster. The word "fool" comes from the Latin *follis* which means "a pair of bellows, a windbag." This description applies to the fool because his or her words are only air and therefore void of meaning. The plural form of *follis* is *folles* meaning "puffed cheeks." An Italian cognate, *buffare*, "to puff," reiterates this characteristic of fools naming them "buffoons." Another connotation of *follis* relates specifically to the scrotum or testicles of the fool.[8] The Italian *coglione*, the Latin *gerro*, and the Sicilian *pudendum*, each allude to the fertility and generating power of the fool.[9] Now we have the fool associated not merely with nonsense but with exaggerated sexuality as well. This provocative nuance alludes to the origin of the European clown in the satyr of Greek comedy which in turn derives from the phallic rituals of Dionysius.[10]

The word "clown" comes from the same source as "farm worker, boor, funny fellow, buffoon, jester."[11] After 1550 the word "clown" appears in English as *cloyne, cloine* or *clowne*. The word "clown" is derived from words meaning "clod," "clot," and "lump." A "clod" is a material formed from coagulated liquid. A congealed mass is a "clot." And a "lump" is something held together very loosely. Although the term "clown" refers to a clod, clot, and lump, a clown can do just the opposite. A clown can be one who melts the taken for granted solidity of the world and its events.[12]

> The clown has the power to surround us with an
> atmosphere of make-believe, in which nothing is
> serious, nothing is solid, nothing has abiding
> consequences. Under the dissolvent influence of his
> personality the iron network of physical, social and
> moral law, which enmeshes us from cradle to grave,
> seems--for the moment--negligible as a web of
> gossamer.[13]

The term "idiot," derived from the Greek *idiotes*,
means a "private person," the ultimate outsider.[14] The
merrymaker, the jester, comes from the French word *geste*
and is related to songs of heroism. When applied to the
fool, it is a mock heroism as in the breaking of a lance
(rather than throwing one), which can be considered the
same as "cracking a joke."[15] The wild man is comparable
to the still extant western notion of "the primitive." The
wild man is the individual in nature. He or she is in
control of the animals and the nature spirits. The wild man
is not just free of all social constraints, he or she is beyond
their bounds.[16] The wild man viewed as a "madman"
displays another nuance on the meaning of the fool.
Madmen were often seen as prophets or oracles with
substantial medical or magical skills, often bringing about
good luck by deflecting the bad.[17] The trickster is
commonly referred to as the spirit of disorder, the mischief
maker, "the Lord of Misrule,"[18] who is very happy to
cause confusion and turmoil. All of these nuanced
meanings behind the term "fool" give us an excellent
picture of the fool's *raison d'être*: to wreck havoc, disrupt
life, mock ways and customs, and generally laugh at social
norms in an effort to relax them to the degree that the fool
is lax in them.

As images of chaos, fools are often described as physically deformed or oddly dressed. Dwarfs and hunchbacks can be fools because their bodies are out of proportion to the norms of physical appearance in the society in which they live. The same is true of men and women dressed in rags, ill-fitting clothes, or garments with a motley design or appearance.[19] Two familiar examples of fools are the court jester with his eared cap and bells and the harlequin with his black face.

Fools are frequently encountered in pairs. They are "doubles," rather than have "doubles." Perhaps the most well-known pair is the king and the court jester. The figure of the king is the one who stands at the center after he has created a kingdom, a cosmos. In the process of creation he has excluded the magical, the demonic, and the natural from his kingdom by setting rigid boundaries. The court jester stands at the edges of this kingdom, this cosmos. He straddles both realms. He is at once the king's conduit to the magical world beyond the boundaries of the kingdom and its intrusion into the kingdom. As the court jester relates to the world beyond the pale, he also relates to the king as the one who acts in his stead as a "mock" king with royal titles to boot. This makes the fool the king's double. In this role, the jester serves to deflect and diminish threats to the power and safety of the king brought about by the forces not always held at bay beyond the kingdom's boundaries by calling them upon him or herself.[20]

Another historical pairing is the wild man and the woman. Fools are sometimes paired with transvestites. Together they are the forces of sexuality, fertility, and the unharnessed, "crazy" vitality of nature. As images of nature, these fools depict life and death as part of the same mystery. And this mystery, like its emissaries, is not subject to the social norms of the day. The fools disrupt the social norms with the insistence that life is the answer to sorrow, sickness, and death. The fool, unlike the hero, never triumphs, because he or she has a double nature which includes the opposites of life and death which cannot be separated.[21] Life cannot destroy death nor death end life. The message which the ritual clowns offer is not one of resolution and completion but of process and renewal. These ritual clowns, these fools, are masks of St. James the Apostle. He represents, like the image of the king, an ordered cosmos, and how life should be: faithful, uncompromising, victorious. The clowns represent the intrusion of chaos and how life really is: ambiguous, ironic, contradictory.[22] In the fiesta, these ritual clowns temporarily displace St. James and substitute their view of reality for his. In place of a saint-king, we have in the *caballero* a mock saint, a court jester, and his double, the *vejigante*, a false adversary. Rather than the *caballero* claiming all goodness as his own and positing the *vejigante* as completely evil, both ritual clowns point to the mystery of our own doubling. We all have good and evil in ourselves. Rather than a saint-hero, we have the *viejo*, who should, as a wild man, be seducing women. It appears that we have an impotent fellow unable to consummate his relationship with his partner, the *loca*, the crazy woman, because of his old age. The nature of these ritual clowns calls our attention back to the theme of renewal in the contradictory notion of "pregnant old age."[23] The *viejo* includes in himself the sexual power of his double, the *loca*. She, in turn, includes the old man as birth-giving death.[24] The life-cycle and the vitality of sexuality is denied and affirmed simultaneously.

THE RITUAL CLOWNS OF LOIZA ALDEA

The ritual clowns reveal that what we take for opposition and conflict on the surface of life conceals a deeper complementarity and doubling in life. The Christian dichotomies of Christ and Satan, good and evil, heaven and hell, represented by Santiago Apóstol appear as doubles as well as opposites in conflict in the ritual clowns. When looking at the first set of ritual clowns, the *caballero* and the *vejigante*, we need to remember how strong the tie is between violence and Spanish piety. Thomas Mitchell tells us that "the Spanish martial spirit is simply indistinguishable from Spanish religiosity." He stresses the symbiotic relationship between violence and piety in Spain as the only way of understanding the conquest of the New World. The conquest is none other than the transformation of the cross of Christ into the dagger and sword hilt.[25] It is easy to see then that a Puerto Rican religious festival can reiterate such a violent theme in its portrayal of the already violent story of *los moros y cristianos* (the Moors and the Christians). But this is only one source of the violence. The other emerges from a fundamental tension within Christianity itself.

The *caballero* and the *vejigante* represent life and the cosmos as a battlefield between opposing forces: good and evil, Christianity and paganism, the Spaniards and the Moors, the master and the slave, Christ and the devil. Today such opposing forces can be construed in more mundane terms as colonizer and colonized, Church and people, rich and poor, male and female. These oppositions make sense because the Christian faith that underlies the fiesta suggests them. Christian cosmology centers upon the person and work of Jesus of Nazareth, the Christ. The Doctrine of the Incarnation, that God descended and became a human being, is Christianity's proclamation that God is involved in history and is not simply an impersonal deity who created the world and then left it to its own devices. Christ's mission, as the New Testament tells us, and as Christian tradition affirms, was to reconcile the world to God after it separated itself from God through the Fall.[26] The story of the Fall recounted in the Book of Genesis[27] alludes to a major theme in Christian thought, the enduring conflict between good and evil. God battles Satan on a cosmic level for the souls of humankind. The battle is won, Christian thought tells us, when Christ, the Mediator, through his violent and bloody death on the cross atones for humankind's original sin of disobedience in the Garden of Eden. Through his self-sacrifice Christ redeems humankind for all times and places. The devil is defeated and Christ is victorious. However, the conflict between good and evil, though conquered on a cosmic level, remains on a historical one. Christian thought tells us that Satan still tempts the individual in everyday life. The individual, then, needs to appeal to Christ for aid in combatting the devil, for assistance in resisting temptation, for the faith to reject sin. So while the heavens are ultimately at peace, the individual in the world is constantly in a state of siege, in a battle against evil. Moreover, the individual's success or failure in combatting the devil has dire ramifications. The ultimate destiny of the human soul is at stake. Those who succeed reap their reward in heaven. Those who fail endure the torments of hell.

When we look at the *caballero* and the *vejigante*, they present us with caricatures of the story. The historical conflict between the Spaniards and the Moors, and the theological opposition between Christ and the devil, are transformed, revealing the concealed doubling of contradiction in the ritual clowns. The *caballero* is a fake. Though dressed up to look like a cavalry soldier, his uniform is obviously more silly than serious. Streaming from his flower bedecked hat are long multicolored ribbons and little bells reminiscent of the get-up of a court jester. His shirt and pants conjure up the image of a harlequin with their checkered design. Most importantly, this "warrior" is without a sword, without a weapon for attack or defense. He is a mock saint, and like one with a the broken lance mentioned above, he is a joke. Without his sword, the *caballero* looks neither Spanish nor Christian. The saint has been uncrowned in the fiesta.

The *vejigante* makes a sham of his alleged Satanic powers. Unlike Satan, the *vejigante* has no voice for persuading innocents to transgress; he can only articulate unintelligible hoots and howls, waving his stick. It is this innocent club used for mock intimidation that gives the *vejigante* his name. Traditionally, his "fool stick" had at the end of it a bladder or *vejiga*. Like the buffoon mentioned above, the *vejigante* and his *vejiga* are full of hot air. With his bicolored tunic, and head full of horns, this devil still manages to dispute with the *caballero* as do court jesters with their kings. And like the proverbial jester, a figure who stands on the boundary, the *vejigante* keeps harm away from the *caballero* by attracting it to himself.

There is no final opposition between these two ritual clowns. We have rather a connection between the two that promises to make the *caballero* look very foolish if he takes the *vejigante*, a jokester, too seriously. As the fiesta shows, the *caballero* does not take the *vejigante* seriously. The *caballero's* mistake is that he takes himself seriously.

The *viejo* and the *loca*, reiterate the tension between the *caballero* and the *vejigante* but on a more domestic level. As the story goes, in the Garden of Eden,

Adam and Eve were tempted by Satan, the personification of evil. Their decision to disobey God, to eat an apple from the Tree of Knowledge, forced God to expel them from Paradise. The burden of humankind's expulsion from Eden falls on Eve's shoulders because she was the first one to eat the fruit at Satan's (the Adversary's) suggestion. Eve may have left Paradise with Adam, but she left separated from him and opposed to him. This separation is symbolized by the association of God with goodness and males on the one hand and by the association of the devil with evil and women on the other. The devil, the *diabolos* (the divider) can bear Eve's likeness, though like the *vejigante*, it is masked. Both Eve and the devil are symbolized by ugly, horned goats, which work like witches whose trickery seduces men into doing evil.[28] But again, the old man and the crazy woman are doubles of each other. Although they both have lost their immunity to the cycle of life and death through their sin, they both retain their place within that same cycle as life-givers.

The view of woman as seductress is common in Puerto Rico as well as in other Hispanic countries. Women are often judged according to their sexual behavior. They can be pure and virginal, good mothers and obedient wives, or seductresses and prostitutes. In keeping with images of immorality and evil, a married woman who enters into an affair is said to "put horns on her husband" (*ponerle los cuernos*).[29] In this way an unfaithful wife makes her husband a "cuckhold," one who is symbolically transformed into a woman, that is, a "goat" who has horns.[30]

The appearance and the antics of the *viejo* and the *loca* are also ludicrous. Today's *viejo* dresses in a sportscoat and necktie. On his head he may wear a fedora or a white wig. A beard or a rubber mask, indicating the wrinkles that come with old age, may cover his face. This

form of his costume is interesting in that it is a literal
translation of the name of this clown--"old man." The
traditional costume of the *viejo* is much more suggestive.
It is from this costume that we can see that the *viejo* is
himself a fool.

This older costume includes a hat, a mask cut out of
a shoe box, shirt, pants, cane and a doll. This disguise
dramatically changes the possible referents for the *viejo*
from the more contemporary guise described above. First,
the clothes are ill-fitting, ragtag, or motley. Second, the
mask suggests the head of an animal in its features. Upon
closer examination, the mask looks like the face of a mule
or donkey. Third, the cane and the doll are instructive. We
have here an almost classically outfitted "wild man," with
disheveled clothes, a face that reminds one of an ass, and
carrying a fool's stick replete with a clown's head or
dummy. All of these accoutrements point to this particular
Puerto Rican example of the fool as wild man.

This insight into the *viejo's* identity has been the
most difficult to discern due to his more modern disguise.
His identity as a wild man or madman links him to the four
ritual clowns in a way that would not be possible otherwise.
The contemporary costume helps to explain why very little
is ever said about the function of the *viejo*. Although the
traditional garb is often mentioned, it is not highlighted. In
the place of costuming are comments related to the
traditional role of what the *viejo* does, namely, provide
music during the fiesta, a task which the *viejo* no longer
performs. As we have seen in the previous chapter, that
function is provided by professional bands.

This change in costume is particularly interesting.
The more contemporary look suggests a *viejo* who is a
venerated personage in Puerto Rican society. Old age, and
the experience that comes with it, has granted him wisdom.

However, in the context of the fiesta, the *viejo* is vulnerable
to parody as one who, in courting the infirmity of old age,
approaches senility, false teeth, and a loss of vision. Not
unlike Eve, who is outside of the kingdom of God due to
her treachery, the *viejo*, like Adam, is a prisoner to life and
the aging process. He has no "bite," nor can he "see" what
future lies before him. He is impotent in every sense of the
word. Together, the *viejo* and the *loca*, express the lot of
humankind after the Fall. They end up constantly making
"fools" out of each other in the proverbial "battle of the
sexes."

In the contemporary context, a "fall" evidences itself
in the dramatic changes in the island's economy. The
traditional economic domains of men, farming and fishing,
have been all but lost in Puerto Rico's movement toward
modernization. And with reverses in the island's progress
toward industrialization during the 1970s, the jobs which
remain are in factories, the service sector, and government.
These positions are primarily targeted toward, and occupied
by, women. This is, in part, because women are considered
to be "more manageable." Often single parents or the
breadwinners in families, women find themselves at the
mercy of management due to their need to work. And
since many women are available for work, their numbers
make them easily replaceable.[31]

In Loíza Aldea today, women support their families
in one light manufacturing job created as a part of Puerto
Rico's economic development program *Fomento*. The
women assemble leather wallets for shipment to the United
States. The men support themselves by making and selling
pitorro, illegal rum.[32] Other family members contribute
by selling fruits, coconuts, and crabs alongside the
highway.[33] So, today's *viejo* wears a commerically made
mask, but as one who has been shut out of commerce. He

wears a mask which he has not made with his two hands as
generations of men before him did. This makes the *viejo*
not only impotent but also "cuckholded" by his place in his
own society. No longer the breadwinner, he has become
like a woman, the traditionally dependent sex in Puerto
Rican society.

The *loca* is a satire on womanhood. Though as a
woman the *loca* is by definition desirable, she is distasteful
to Puerto Rican society because, like Eve, she flaunts
herself rather than maintaining the more customary modesty
befitting women. The *loca* is a flirt. She parades down the
route of the religious processions more like a prostitute,
soliciting attentions, than like one of the young women and
girls who have been elevated to the status of *reinas*
(queens) and *reinas infantiles* (child queens) of the fiesta.
But again, we will see that there is no real opposition here.
Both the *viejo* and the *loca* are marginal characters at the
farthest edge of social respectability. Like the *caballero*
and the *vejigante*, they, too, occupy a place on the
boundary.

The House and the Street

In order to understand the *loca* better, we need to
look at the two basic social domains of Loíza Aldea, the
house and the street.[34] The house, or more appropriately
the home, is the traditional social domain of women,
daughters, wives, and mothers. The home is where the
children are born and reared, making it the place of
biological (childbirth) and social (childrearing) reproduction.
The objects of this world, the household implements such
as the broom, stand for a woman's prominence in the home.
They are emblems of her power to order her world.
Cleaning, after all, is the elimination of dirt. Dirt, however,

is more than mud, sand, and dust. It is, according to Mary
Douglas, "essentially disorder," "matter out of place."[35]
The woman who cleans her home is organizing her
environment; she is creating a world.
The street is the traditional social domain of men.
As the street is separate from the home, it underscores more
than a traditional separation between male and female
worlds. This separation, like that of the sheep from the
goats,[36] has a ring of finality about it. The street includes
a man's work, his productive activity, as he increasingly
must commute to work on highways since he can no longer
work in the sugarcane fields as did so many generations of
men before him. It also connotes a man's social life as he
gathers on the street to play dominoes, or in taverns, to talk
with his fellows about his *amantes* (lovers).[37] A man's
social life, then, is not confined to his friends but also
includes possible and realized extramarital liaisons with
women.

In Puerto Rican and other Hispanic cultures, this
aspect of a man's social life is called *donjuanismo*, a gloss
on *machismo* which emphasizes "sexual freedom, virility,
and aggressiveness for men in contrast to women's sexual
repression, feminity, and passivity."[38] As Peggy Reeves
Sanday has persuasively argued, an emphasis on a woman's
femininity and passivity in sexual matters spills over into
her economic concerns as well. Her gender, historically,
binds a woman in western cultures to her domestic role
even in the workplace.[39]

In the early patriarchal, paternalistic, and military
society of Puerto Rico, women were subordinant and
assigned the role of maintaining the institution of the
family. Women were to be "obedient daughters, faithful
wives, devoted mothers" and nothing more.[40] Perhaps
Stan Steiner is correct when he says that the Spanish

conquest of the New World was a conquest of the women.[41] Women were literally put in their place and forced to stay there by the domestic violence of social convention.

With the uneasy transition from an agricultural economy, the domain of men, to an industrial one in the late nineteenth century, women entered the workforce in order to feed their families as their men were often out of work. As a reservoir of cheap labor, women discovered that only certain jobs were open to them because of strict divisions of labor based upon sex. Not surprisingly, women were most often employed in jobs related to their domestic domain--needlecrafts (including the garment industry), domestic service, and clerical work. Moreover, since men still dominated the culture (although agricultural jobs were hard to find), a working woman's wages were considered to be "supplementary."

> The results were predictable; the cycle unbroken. This 'supplementary' role has been used to justify the continued inequality in wages for men and women, as well as occupational segregation in low-paying, unskilled jobs in the manufacturing, clerical, and service sectors.[42]

This confirms Peggy Reeves Sanday's thesis: "No matter how it is produced, sexual separation (for whatever reason) creates two worlds--one male and the other female, each consisting of a system of meanings and a program of behavior."[43]

What, then, does today's *loca* have to say to us regarding the two social domains? The traditional *loca* mirrored the woman of the house in organizing her environment. Her gesture of sweeping the streets during the fiesta was a symbolic way of eliminating evil, sin, and bad luck, as the woman sweeping her house "cleans" her home.[44] This activity in the context of the fiesta extends the domain of the woman into the spiritual and presents us with a connection between the home and the church. As she takes care of her home, the woman as *loca* cares for the street. In this sense she can be construed as a healer.[45] Moreover, the church is viewed as domestic by nature, making it inherently unmasculine. As we noted in the previous chapter, homes serve as house-churches for the nine days of novenas celebrated before the fiesta. Homes are also places where the images of Santiago Apóstol are lovingly cared for during the year.

During the fiesta's religious processions, we see the interpenetration of the two basic domains. We see women carrying both the image which is for them, *Santiago de las mujeres*, and *Santiaguito*, the image dedicated to their children. When the statues are moved from their homes to the cork tree at *Las Carreras,* the members of the procession salute not only each individual statue as it joins the procession, but they also salute the homes and the *matenadoras* (guardians) of those statues. This is because the role of guardian of a statue carries with it enormous prestige and power as we saw in chapter three.

We also saw in the previous chapter on the fiesta and its religious processions that the image of Santiago Apóstol generates a new social domain. This domain is created by the penetration of the street by the house. The images of the saint come out of the homes of the *matenadoras* into the public eye, and the homes of the villagers are open to the street in that visitors are welcomed inside for refreshment. While it can be argued that the street is domesticated during the fiesta,[46] it is equally true that the religious processions are "outdoor events," liturgies of the streets, where men can feel comfortable, identify

with the Saint, and be free of priestly (domestic) control.[47]
This new domain does not represent a change in the status
of men and women. It is a "demilitarized zone." This new
domain serves to neutralize the traditional male and female
roles and conflicts for a brief time. As the ritual clowns
become less and less normative in their social behavior, the
more expressive and symbolic they become.[48]

Into this new domain comes the *loca*, a mixture of
wife and mother (*la mujer buena o de la casa*), and
prostitute, the woman of the street (*la mujer mala o de la
calle*).[49] The clue to this double identification is the
symbol associated with virtuous housewives and cunning
witches--the broom.

> The humble broomstick has played an intriguing part
> in the social, sexual and psychic life of mankind. In
> popular belief witches invariably fly through the air
> on broomsticks, though in fact the number of witches
> who confessed to doing so is remarkably small.
> Brooms were originally made of a stalk of the broom
> plant with a bunch of leaves at the head. As an
> indoor, domestic implement, the broom became a
> symbol of woman.[50]

When the broom is removed from the house and
taken into the street, the man's domain is penetrated by the
woman's domain. Here we have a stunning example of the
kind of reversal made common by fools. They dislocate
things in order for us to see them differently. The result of
this topsy-turvy situation is that the broom, along with the
loca, becomes a symbol of illicit, that is, uncontrollable,
and therefore threatening, female sexuality. When *locas*
appear, they show on the one hand how foolish men look
in the traditional attire (domain) of women, and on the
other hand,[51] how promiscuous and immoral women are,

by definititon, when they enter the domain of men (the street). We can see this more clearly when we look at the traditional association of a woman's sexual appetite with her broomstick.

> According to tradition, witches rode through the air with broomsticks between their legs, en route to the witches' sabbath. [...] the broomstick is a euphemism for the male penis, in much the same way that the maypole is also a symbol of fertility.[52]

One might pose the question, when a witch has a broomstick between her legs, has she taken the symbolic penis *on* or *in*? In the normative sense, a woman with a penis between her legs would be said to have taken the penis in. The *loca*, it could be argued, has also taken it on, as she invades the street, the masculine domain, brandishing her broom. As in the sexual act, the symbolic penis, the broom, is a link between the sexes which both attaches them and keeps them apart. It is this kind of simultaneous attachment and separation that characterizes the *loca's* double nature as a ritual clown. In her, gender conflict and complementarity exist side-by-side.

Today's *locas* represent a reinterpretation of the tradition. Interpreted as homosexuals by the youth of Loíza Aldea,[53] the *locas* at the fiesta in 1986 were portrayed by gay males from San Juan.[54] With the symbolism of the broom in mind, it makes a great deal of sense for a homosexual male, who is often seen as carrying within himself the same gender dualism, to adopt the character of the *loca* rather than take on as his own the identity of one of the other ritual clowns. Though the actual broom is now missing from the fiesta, the homosexual male as *loca*, in his sexual preference, recalls the female sexual role symbolized by the broom.

The *loca* attracts smiles and laughter from onlookers, but her transvestite appearance in the street is no laughing matter. In western cultures, men can be very afraid of women.

> Creation metaphors for male dominance resolve tensions between opposing forces and conflicting wills. Described within the context of sex-role behavior, these metaphors express the psychological bed-rock of male dominance. Men fear, envy, and oppress women.[55]

As we see from the important work of Peggy Reeves Sanday,[56] creation or origin myths mirror the separation between the sexes. Since the myth of the Garden of Eden women have shared a common identity with the devil in western culture, finding themselves defined as seductresses and manipulators.

The Hispanic adoption and adaptation of this creation myth is instructive for understanding the deep-seated threat inherent in the *loca*. We have discussed the dual nature of women, commenting specifically on how women, through their dominance of men, can symbolically transform men into women. This is precisely the threat the *loca* presents. Whether or not she is portrayed by a homosexual male, the result is the same. The broom symbolizes the threat of anal penetration, "to take it by the ass" (*tomarlo por culo*).[57] The laughter evoked by the *loca* is in direct proportion to how seriously her challenge is taken.[58]

It is very curious to note that no one seems to know when the *viejo* and the *loca* became a regular part of the fiesta. To some their roots can be found in the traditional carnivals of Spain.[59] And when I ask Pastora Carrasquillo,

the wife of the deceased Loiceño mask maker Don Castor
Ayala, about the *viejos* and the *locas*, she will tell me only
what they look like; that is, what they used to look like
when Alegría did his first work on Loíza Aldea in the late
1940s. Perhaps the inability to date the appearance of these
two figures accurately tells us how deeply the "Old Man"
and the "Crazy Woman" are rooted in the Western mind.
Admittedly, this is speculation. I am suggesting that the
juxtaposition of the "Old Man" and the "Crazy Woman" is
a root paradigm,"[60] an image of ourselves so taken for
granted, so much a part of *our* make-up, that we cannot see
it as a mask.

The discomfort that these masked figures can arouse
in the populace is hidden by the humor they evoke. It is at
the moment when our laughter accompanies the subversive
antics of the masked figures that the potential for rethinking
social structures occurs. Humor is the reaction we have to
any implausible possibility for social relations.[61]   As
tricksters, the *caballero*, the *vejigante*, the *viejo*, and the
loca are deformed characters who disrupt the social order
while at the same time hinting at the possibilities of a larger
reformation of society. It is just this possibility of
alteration, this "alternative pattern which makes sense to a
sufficient degree for it to be entertained momentarily as a
new and creative combination" that induces laughter.[62]
Yet both the laughter and the possibility for substantive
change are as transitory as the ritual clowns themselves.

MASKED MISCHIEF MAKERS

The fiesta of Santiago Apóstol is more than just an
annual commemoration of a patron saint. It is a text that
can be read.[63] This text is a condensed and polysemic

statement about how the pueblo of Loíza Aldea sees itself.
The fiesta tells us in miniature, through its constellation of
sacred symbols, the generalities that make up Loíza Aldea's
self-understanding. What appears obvious on the surface
may look quite different when its roots are revealed.

Central to this self-disclosure is the symbol of
Santiago Apóstol that dominates the fiesta. He is its focus.
As the fiesta's foremost sacred symbol, Santiago Apóstol
presents to the people of Loíza Aldea a worldview; that is,
a comprehensive definition of reality. The worldview
symbolized by Santiago Apóstol is this: that good triumphs
over evil and that the original order of creation is restored.
This theme of restoration or re-creation finds its origins in
the Spanish conquest of the Moors and the victory of Christ
over the devil.

A worldview does not exist for itself. It is one half of
a process of making sense out the world in which one lives.
The other half is the ethos of a community. The worldview
provides an interpretation of the world while the ethos is
the way one moves through the world. The salient
characteristic of this process is that both worldview and
ethos mutually reiterate and reinforce each other. Whatever
is believed about the world sets the boundaries for conduct
in the community. Whatever parameters are set for
behavior authenticate the view of the world. This dialectic
results in a believable world and a code of conduct that is
meaningful. Both the intellect and the emotions are
satisfied. The way life is portrayed and the way life is
lived are seen as real and necessary, respectively. Both the
worldview and ethos are embodied in, even fused with, the
sacred symbols of the community, and it is in these sacred
symbols that a worldview and an ethos are appropriated by
a community.

> Such religious symbols, dramatized in rituals or
> related in myths, are felt somehow to sum up, for
> those whom they are resonant, what is known about
> the way the world is, the quality of the emotional life
> it supports, and the way one ought to behave while in
> it. Sacred symbols thus relate an ontology and a
> cosmology to an aesthetics and a morality. Their
> particular power comes from their presumed ability to
> identify fact with the value at the most fundamental
> level, to give what is otherwise merely actual, a
> comprehensive normative import.[64]

Though the dominant symbol in the fiesta, Santiago Apóstol
is part of a larger constellation of symbols operative in the
fiesta. These others are instrumental symbols. Like
dominant symbols, instrumental symbols are symbols which
must be interpreted in terms of their relations with the other
symbols within the fiesta. They are the means by which we
come to grasp who Santiago Apóstol is and how Loíza
Aldea sees itself.

The instrumental symbols in the fiesta are the ritual
clowns: the *caballero*, the *vejigante*, the *viejo*, and the
loca. They are not the end point of the fiesta.[65] They are
interpretive guides in the search for Santiago Apóstol's
underlying meaning, for the meaning of Santiago Apóstol
is found more fully in concert with the ritual clowns than
in the dominant symbol of Santiago Apóstol alone.

Since dominant symbols are highly condensed, they
are capable of holding together many different referents as
do the ritual clowns. The ritual clowns are united to
Santiago Apóstol in that they flesh out the story of his
victory of the Spanish over the Moors in more
contemporary and immediate terms. They refer, as does the
symbol of Santiago Apóstol, to a worldview and an ethos

that gives rise to emotion.[66] For example, the ritual
clowns often evoke fear in little children and laughter in
adults.

The cluster of the four ritual clowns as instrumental
symbols in the fiesta do more than just refer to the ultimate
restoration of creation mirrored in Santiago Apóstol. They
re-create it, but in a different way. They poke fun at the
sacred symbol of Santiago Apóstol and the boundaries that
it creates.

These ritual clowns are tricksters who challenge the
generally accepted worldview and its accompanying ethos.
While on the one hand, they reinforce the symbol of
Santiago Apóstol with its view of conflict and contradiction
in the fiesta's characterizations of soldier against enemy and
male against female, they also resist it. Although their
message may be momentary and their insights never
institutionalized, the importance of these tricksters in the
fiesta cannot be overestimated, for there is a contrarian
impulse in these ritual clowns. They resist the
generalizations presented by the symbol of Santiago
Apóstol. They are deconstructive. Rather than accept the
fiesta's worldview and ethos at face value, the *caballero*,
the *vejigante*, the *viejo*, and the *loca* take them on, they
wear them as masks. They really mimic the model of
conflict inherent in Santiago Apóstol's symbol and turn it
upside down. They show us how life really is. They reveal
the complementarity which is concealed underneath the
conflict. The ritual clowns hold within themselves a double
nature which holds conflict and complementarity together.

Each masked fool does this by putting on the face
of another. Ordinary people become soldier-saints, fiendish
devils, silly old men, and scandalous women. Ordinary
people temporarily suspend their own social roles in order
to comprehend the other through mimicry. As tricksters,

the ritual clowns can do this because they cross boundaries, or stand on boundaries, thereby including in themselves their opposites. This is possible because there are no absolutes, only anomalies and ambiguities for a trickster. They, at one and the same time, withdraw from the prevailing social order and confront it.[67] This is their double character. They are both part of the system and not part of it. Tricksters can debunk the claims of their society's worldview and ethos as fictive because they know them intimately. In their place, they "make up" alternative realities; they wear them as masks on their faces.

The Puerto Rican experience of slavery offers another context for the ritual clowns. We know that the slave masters treated the slaves in the Caribbean as fools. The slaves, in turn, adopted the caricature, using it as a mask behind which they struggled to preserve their own cultural identity.[68] Torn from their familiar social structures, the slaves held on to their myths and rituals thanks to 1) what Roger Bastide calls the "schematic similarities"[69] of the religious systems involved, and 2) "the persistence of culture"[70] extolled by Gordon K. Lewis. The similarities allowed the spirits which accompanied the slaves during the middle passage to find "niches" into which they could insinuate themselves and continue.[71] Cultural persistence is the recognition of the living quality of the religions involved. Lewis even goes so far as to locate the origins of the Caribbean's fierce pride in its indigenous Indians.[72] In part, out of this interpenetration of cultures generated by slavery emerged the ritual clowns of Loíza Aldea.

African Tricksters

The main African influence in Loíza Aldea is that of

the Yoruba culture of West Africa.[73] The African tradition of the Yoruba people shares the notion of the trickster with the European. This is particularly clear in the Yoruba spirit *Eshu/Elegbara*. Like his European counterpart, *Eshu/Elegbara* is a trickster who disrupts the social order. In so doing, he shows himself to be an exemplar of his social order rather than its hero.[74] As an exemplar, he is constantly revealing the realities of lived experience. He brings out into the open all of the ambiguity which characterizes the social order. This revelation is not only disruptive, it is constructive as well. It is constructive because disruption demands communication with the offended spirit. This communication takes place through divination.

Divination is a practice, not of discerning the future, but of interpreting the present by referring to the past stories of the spirits. It uncovers the forces at work within a social conflict, is the means by which these forces can be reconciled, and is the passageway to the order hidden in the conflict.[75] The process of divination begins when there is a recognized conflict within the social order. This conflict is symbolized as an offense to a spirit. The offended spirit is identified by the telling of stories, the collection of the condensed wisdom of the people. These stories tell of problems and their resolution. They also tell of what happens when the appropriate sacrifice is not performed. Restoration happens when the sacrifice is made.

Eshu/Elegbara is a part of the Yoruba divination process called *Ifá*. He is an agent of the shattering and rebuilding of worlds.[76] *Eshu/Elegbara*, the messenger of the spirits, brought *Ifá*, the Yoruba way of knowledge, to the world. It is through *Eshu/Elegbara,* the breaker of boundaries, that *Ifá* dissolves the present order and redefines it, that is, by revealing the course which must be

Santiago por los hombres

Santiago por las mujeres

Flag bearers salute each other

Four Caballeros and a Vejigante

Two Viejos

Two Locas hug

A Vejigante spreads his wings

Three Young Caballeros

A Loca puts an arm around a friend as a Viejo stands by

followed in life.[77] *Eshu/Elegbara,* "the anger of the gods," stirs up trouble so that sacrifice will be offered. In this way, the order of the spirits is made available to humankind. *Eshu/Elegbara* is a mischievous figure. Because he likes to stir up trouble, he has erroneously been likened to the Christian personification of evil, Satan. *Eshu/Elegbara*

is certainly not the Devil of our New Testament acquaintance, who is an out and out evil power in opposition to the plan of God's salvation for man. On the whole, it would be near the truth to parallel him with Satan in the Book of Job [1:6ff], where Satan is one of the ministers of God and has the office of trying men's sincerity and putting their religion to the proof.[78]

It is *Eshu/Elegbara's* job to report to *Olodumare,* the Great God of Yoruba belief, the comings and goings of humankind, especially with regard to its worship and offerings. He delivers these offerings to *Olodumare* and punishes the lazy when their offerings are unacceptable or insufficient. *Eshu/Elegbara* can do this because *Olodumare* has given him the power to build up and the power to tear down. *Eshu/Elegbara* stands at the crossroads between the spirits and humankind.

So, *Eshu/Elegbara* is the master of the destiny of men and women. While *Eshu/Elegbara* is constantly stirring up trouble as in the famous story of his cap with many colors,[79] his constantly erect penis reminds us of all of the possibilites in life. With this penis, and a trick or two, *Eshu/Elegbara* can, and does, take any woman he wants to bed, be she married or single. His sexual escapades break all boundaries and then redefine them.

The old man in some parts of the new world and the

lecher in the old, *Eshu/Elegbara* is a very interesting fellow. He is the "owner of the power," the "ultimate master of potentiality."[80] His àshé[81] is the power to break down or multiply all events.[82] *Eshu/Elegbara* teaches the "lesson of the crossroads," that is,

> knowing what is truth and what is falsehood [...] the point where doors open and close, where persons have to make decisions that may forever affect their lives...[83]

We can see this in the *caballero* and the *vejigante*. In the *caballero* and the *vejigante* we have a parable of war. But this one comes with a twist like the work of *Eshu/Elegbara*. With the *caballero*, the lack of weaponry is no accident. It is the ancient wisdom of the fools in the fiesta that the one who unsheaths his sword can just as easily turn it on himself as on another. Or, perhaps more to the point, that turning one's sword on the other is tantamount to turning it on oneself in the end. Marcel Mauss argued many years ago that competition without conflict could be maintained through an exchange system called "potlatch," a kind of one-upmanship in gift-giving. If people spent their time exchanging gifts with open hands, he argued, they would not be grasping their weapons in their hands. In this way, they could "oppose one another without slaughter and give without sacrificing themselves to others."[84]

It is a similar view of social relationships that the *viejo* and the *loca* contest. Like the *caballero* and the *vejigante*, the *viejo* and the *loca* offer us an opportunity to reflect upon and reconsider the social order. Here we have the breaking open of possibilities which characterizes the work of *Eshu/Elegbara*.

Take, for example, the *viejo* whom I saw at the

fiesta in the summer of 1986. He was dressed in a false white beard, fedora, sportscoat and briefcase. On the side of the briefcase were the neatly stenciled letters "F.B.I." Whatever one's political leanings, this *viejo* was commenting upon the social and political structure that had an agency of the United States government watching and judging the behavior of Puerto Ricans. This *viejo* was calling into question the unbalanced patriarchal structure which made Puerto Rico, like the woman in the Christian creation myth, the inferior, incapable of living her own life well.

Or take the *loca* whom I saw that same summer. She was portrayed by a male homosexual dressed in women's clothing. This was not an example of saturnalian offensiveness, but rather the result of the power of ritual. Today's gay males, who are "dirt" in their own society, take on the posture of women who are themselves unequal to men. Though sadly foolish, today's gay male takes on the role of the subservient woman in Puerto Rican society. In so doing he not only questions that role, but he also inverts his own status, making for himself a temporary place among those who ordinarily revile him. Though unacceptable as himself, the homosexual male, as *loca*, is tolerated.

This leveling of oppositional postures is part of the hypothetical or subjunctive process of the fiesta. It allows the four ritual clowns, after the manner of *Eshu/Elegbara*, to call into question with a sanctioned disrespect[85] the view of reality and life represented by the symbol of Santiago Apóstol. They get away with it because their challenge to Santiago Apóstol is humorous. It is ludicrous. It is recreation.

By poking fun at the dominant symbol of the fiesta, the *caballero*, the *vejigante*, the *viejo*, and the *loca* are playful in their response to life's travails. They challenge our daily understanding of life and offer us a glimpse at higher realities and new possibilities. In the re-creation of the fiesta of Santiago Apóstol, the four masked figures deconstruct the taken-for-granted social relationships that created them, and put in their place a partial picture of what a new order of existence might look like, an order based upon an acceptance of ambiguity rather than an absolute opposition between good and evil.

CONCLUSION

Santiago Apóstol came to the New World with the Spanish ships that sailed to the West Indies in search of gold. The name of the transplanted patron saint of Spain was invoked in the New World much as it had been in Spain during the years of the Reconquest. So it is in his role as liberator and defender that he is depicted in the statues carried during the fiesta held in his honor in Loíza Aldea.

And yet to grasp the meaning of this particular Santiago Apóstol, we have had to look not only at his image rendered in the statues of him which reiterate in their details his Iberian legend, but also at the ritual clowns of the fiesta, the *caballero*, the *vejigante*, the *viejo* and the *loca*. It is through these instrumental symbols which hold within themselves an ironic view of life that we can see the true face of the Santiago Apóstol of Loíza Aldea and, in turn, how Loíza Aldea paints its own face as a community. My contention is that these condensed portraits of Santiago Apóstol and Loíza Aldea are one and the same. *Loíza está de fiesta.* (Loíza is about the fiesta.)[86] To gain access to these images, we focused on the three days of religious procession in the fiesta in the previous chapter, for in these processions we become pilgrims. We symbolically walk back to the mouth of the *Río Grande de Loíza*, back to the Taíno Arawak *yucayeques*, back to the days of the Spanish settlements, to the slave ships, back to the place where the first statue of Santiago Apóstol appeared.

In recent years the fiesta, a once solemn religious event recalling the heroism of a Spanish saint, is said by some to have taken on a carnival atmosphere. The streets of Loíza Aldea no longer seem to some to rehearse a past victory so much as to ritualize comic behavior. This need not, however, be counted as a loss or intrusion. Nor need we view any part of Loíza Aldea's fiesta as one in need of salvaging. Rather, I view the changes in the fiesta as transitions made possible by the ritual process itself. Sacred symbols are always negotiating with the social structure, searching out "niches" wherein they can survive, and in the process, reconstitute themselves while changing the social structure as well.[87] It may well be that different costumed characters will one day replace the *caballero*, *vejigante*, *viejo*, and *loca* as we know them.[88] Some of this we know has already happened with the *viejo* and the *loca*. But this concern about appearances does not alter the tradition of merrymaking. The perceived change in the fiesta, that is from a solemn religious observance to an frenzied carnival, is in keeping with the attitude of fools. They mock the seriousness of events. In so doing they allow some of the vitality of life to seep through the cracks in the kingdom's walls.

These interjections of novelty, if you will, point to the power inherent in the multivalent symbols of Santiago Apóstol to pull apart the fiesta and then reconstruct it. Ritual offers us the recognition that fiestas are not fixed or immutable but socially and historically mediated. Ritual offers us generalities like Santiago Apóstol in need of specific contexts. Rituals like this Puerto Rican fiesta for Santiago Apóstol accommodate specific applications of the story of *los moros y cristianos* and readies them for interpretations that stay close to the processional route. This is why the ritual clowns in the fiesta are so interesting. Not only recalling the characters familiar to the Hispanic mind, these distinctively Puerto Rican clowns are capable of carrying within themselves associations of much broader significance because they are open to new possibilities. They offer new revelations in their revelry. Mary Douglas puts it this way: "By revealing the arbitrary, provisional nature of the very categories of thought, by lifting the pressure for a moment and suggesting other ways of structuring reality, the joke rite in the middle of sacred moments of religion hints at unfathomable mysteries."[89]

NOTES

1. Judi Young-Laughlin and Charles D. Laughlin, "How Masks Work, Or Masks Work How?", *Journal of Ritual Studies* 2 (Winter 1988): 61.

2. See David Napier, "Festival Masks: A Typology," in *Time Out of Time: Essays on the Festival*, ed. Alessandro Falassi, Albuquerque: University of New Mexico Press, 1967, 211-219; Angelina Pollak-Eltz, "Masks and Masquerade in Venezuela," in *The Power of Symbols: Masks and Masquerade in the Americas*, ed. N. Ross Crumrine and Marjorie Halpin, Vancouver: University of British Columbia Press, 1983, 220; Steven V. Lutes, "The Mask and Magic of the Yaqui Paskola Clowns," in *Ibid.*, 83; and Samuel Glotz, "European Masks," *Drama Review* 26 (Winter 1982), 16.

3. Ronald L. Grimes, *Beginnings in Ritual Studies* (Washington, D.C.: University Press of America, 1982), 75-84.

4. Don Handelman, "The Ritual Clown: Attributes and Affinties," *Anthropos* 76 (1981): 323-324, and N. Ross Crumrine, "Capakoba, The Mayo Easter Ceremonial Impersonator: Explanations of Ritual Clowning," *Journal for the Scientific Study of Religion* 8 (Spring 1969): 10-21.

5. *Ibid.*

6. Handelman, 323.

7. *Ibid.*, 330.

8. William Willeford, *The Fool and His Scepter: A Study in Clowns and Jesters and Their Audience* (Evanston, Illinois: Northwestern University Press, 1969), 10-11.

9. Handelman, 329.

10. Willeford, 10-11.

11. *Ibid.*, 12.

12. Handelman, 328.

13. Enid Welsford, *The Fool: His Social and Literary History* (New York: Farrar & Rinehart, n.d.), 317.

14. Willeford, 13.

15. *Ibid.*

16. *Ibid.*, 79-80.

17. Welsford, 91-92.

18. *Ibid.*, 197.

19. *Ibid.*, 14-16.

20. *Ibid.*, 151-173.

21. *Ibid.*, 174-191.

22. Louis A. Hieb, "Meaning and Mismeaning: Toward an Understanding of the Ritual Clown" in *New Perspectives on the Pueblos*, ed. Alfonso Ortiz (Albuquerque, New Mexico: University of New Mexico Press, 1972), 177.

23. Mikhail Bakhtin, *Rabelais and His World*, trans. Helene Iswolsky, (Cambridge, Massachusetts: The M.I.T. Press, 1968), 352.

24. *Ibid.*, 405.

25. Thomas Mitchell, *Violence and Piety in Spanish Folklore* (Philadelphia: University of Pennsylvania Press, 1988), 29.

26. John 3:16

27. See chapter 3.

28. Andreas Lommel, *Masks: Their Meaning and Function*, trans. Nadia Fowler (New York: McGraw-Hill Book Co., 1972), 197.

29. Edna Acosta-Belén, "Puerto Rican Women in Culture, History, and Society" in *The Puerto Rican Woman: Perspectives in Culture, History, and Society*, 2d ed., ed. Edna Acosta-Belén (New York: Praeger Publishers, 1986), 17.

30. Stanley Brandes, *Metaphors of Masculinity: Sex and Status in Andalusian Folklore* (Philadelphia, Pennsylvania: University of Pennsylvania Press, 1980), 90-91. Cuckholdry is another form of uncrowning according to Bahktin, p. 241.

31. "Inside Puerto Rico 1984: Colonialism and Intervention in the Caribbean and Central America," *Prisa International: Publication of the National Ecumenical Movement of Puerto Rico (PRISA)* 7 (April 1984), 6.

32. David Ungerlieder Kepler, *Fiestas Afro-Boricanas y Cambio Social en Puerto Rico: El Caso de Loíza* (Mexico: Escuela Nacional de Antropología e Historia, M.A. Thesis, 1983), 64.

33. *Ibid.*, 72.

34. My first exposure to this idea of social domains was in reading Roberto DaMatta, "Carnival in Multiple Planes,"in *Rite, Drama, Festival, Spectacle: Rehearsals Toward a Theory of Cultural Performance*, ed. John J. MacAloon (Philadelphia: Institute for the Study of Human Issues, Inc., 1984), 208-240. Other excellent statements can be found in John M. Ingham, *Mary, Michael, and Lucifer: Folk Catholicism in Central Mexico* (Austin: University of Texas Press, 1986), 56-77; in Stanley Brandes, *Metphors of Masculinity: Sex and Status in Andalusian Folklore* (Philadelphia, Pennsylvania: University of Pennsylvania Press, 1980), 137-158, 177-204; and in Peggy Reeves Sanday, *Female Power and Male Dominance: On the Origins of Sexual Inequality* (Cambridge: Cambridge University Press), 1981.

35. Mary Douglas, *Purity and Danger: An Analysis of the Concepts of Pollution and Taboo* (London: Routledge & Kegan Paul, 1966), 2,35.

36. Matthew 25:31-35. Men are traditionally associated with sheep and women with goats.

37. Conversation with Dr. Carmen Collazo, July 1986.

38. Acosta-Belén, 16.

39. Peggy Reeves Sanday, *Female Power and Male Dominance: On the Origins of Sexual Inequality* (Cambridge: Cambridge University Press, 1981), 73.

40. Acosta-Belén, 3.

41. Stan Steiner, *The Islands: The Worlds of the Puerto Ricans* (New York: Harper and Row, Publishers, 1974), 33.

42. Helen I. Safa, "Female Employment and the Social Reproduction of the Puerto Rican Working Class," in Acosta-Belén, 88.

43. Sanday, 7.

44. Alegría, xx.

45. More will be said about healers in the next chapter when I discuss the *bohique*, the Taíno Arawak Indian "doctor."

46. DaMatta, 221.

47. Brandes, 202-203.

48. Conversation with Roberto DaMatta, February 1989.

49. Acosta-Belén, 16.

50. *Man, Myth, & Magic: The Illustrated Encyclopedia of Mythology, Religion and the Unknown*, 12 vols., ed. Richard Cavendish (New York: Marshall Cavendish, 1983), V, 350.

51. Remember that the *locas* are transvestites.

52. Nevill Drury, *Dictionary of Mysticism and the Occult* (San Francisco: Harper and Row, Publishers, 1985), 34.

53. *Las Fiestas de Santiago Apóstol en Loíza*, produced by Ramón H. Almodóvar and Jaime Hamilton Márquez and directed by Luis Martínez Sosa, 57 min., Producciones Vejigante, Inc. and La Fundación de las Humanidades Puertorriqueñas, 1982. Videocassette.

54. This observation was made by Ricardo E. Alegría in January 1988.

55. Sanday, 50.

56. *Ibid.*, 35.

57. Brandes, 95.

58. *Ibid.*, 97.

59. In an interview with Ricardo E. Alegría in January 1988, he made this point.

60. This concept comes from Victor W. Turner. Root paradigms are cultural models for behavior which are not consciously grasped. They deal with fundamental assumptions and are allusive, implicit, and metaphorical. They are axiomatic. See Victor W. Turner and Edith Turner, *Image and Pilgrimage in Christian Culture* (New York: Columbia University Press, 1978), 248-249.

61. Alfonso Ortiz, 135-162.

62. Louis A. Hieb, "Meaning and Mismeaning: Toward an Understanding of the Ritual Clown," in Ortiz, 190.

63. Clifford Geertz, "Deep Play: Notes on a Balinese Cockfight" in *The Interpretation of Cultures: Selected Essays* (New York: Basic Books, 1973), 452.

64. Clifford Geertz, "Ethos, World View, and the Analysis of Sacred Symbols," in *The Interpretation of Cultures: Selected Essays* (New York: Basic Books, 1973), 127.

65. Victor W. Turner, *The Forest of Symbols: Aspects of Ndembu Ritual* (Ithaca, N.Y.: Cornell University Press, 1967), 31.

66. Victor W. Turner, *The Forest of Symbols*, 27-32 and Victor W. Turner and Edith Turner, *Image and Pilgrimage in Christian Culture* (New York: Columbia University Press, 1978), 244-248.

67. Barbara A. Babcock, "Arrange Me into Disorder: Fragments and Reflections on Ritual Clowning," in *Rite, Drama, Festival, Spectacle: Rehearsals Toward a Theory of Cultural Performance*, ed. John J. MacAloon (Philadelphia: Institute for the Study of Human Issues, 1984), 116.

68. Gordon K. Lewis, *Main Currents in Caribbean Thought: The Historical Evolution of Caribbean Society in Its Ideological Aspects, 1492-1900* (Baltimore: The Johns Hopkins University Press, 1983), 182.

69. Roger Bastide, *The African Religions of Brazil: Toward a Sociology of the Interpenetration of Civilizations*, trans. Helen Sebba (Baltimore: The Johns Hopkins University Press, 1960), 161.

70. Lewis, 22.

71. Bastide, 159-160.

72. Lewis, 38-42.

73. Alegría, *La Fiesta de Santiago Apóstol en Loíza Aldea*, 22.

74. Robert D. Pelton, *The Trickster in West Africa: A Study of Mythic Irony and Sacred Delight* (Berkeley: University of California Press, 1980), 227.

75. *Ibid.*, 115.

76. *Ibid.*, 274.

77. *Ibid.*, 152.

78. E. Bolaji Idowu, *Olódùmarè: God in Yoruba Belief* (New York: Frederick A. Praeger, Publishers, 1963), 80.

79. "Once two friends owned adjoining farms. They dressed alike and were in all ways a model of friendship. Eshu decided to make them differ. He used to walk each morning on the path between the two farms, and one day set out wearing a multi-colored cap, variously described as red and white; red, white, and blue; or red, white, green, and black. He also put his pipe at the nape of his neck instead of in his mouth, and let his staff hang over his back instead of his chest. He greeted the friends, already working in their fields, and passed on. Later they began to argue about the color of his cap and which way he was going. [...] Soon they came to blows. When they were brought

before the king, Eshu confessed to igniting the quarrel because 'sowing dissension is my great delight.' When the king tried to bind Eshu, he fled, started a fire in the bush, hurled burning grass on the town, and then mixed up the possessions that townsfolk hauled out of their houses. A dreadful row began, and as Eshu ran off laughing, he boasted that everyone had played his game well." *Ibid.*, 141.

80. Robert Farris Thompson, *Flash of the Spirit: African and Afro-American Art and Philosophy* (New York: Random House, 1983), 19.

81. The word *àshé* means "spiritual command, the power-to-make-things-happen, God's own enabling light rendered to men and women." It is a vital force that is embodied in the spirits. *Ibid.*, 5.

82. *Ibid.*, 23.

83. *Ibid.*, 19.

84. Marcel Mauss, *The Gift: Forms and Functions of Exchange in Archaic Societies*, trans. Ian Cunnison (New York: W.W. Norton and Co., Inc., 1967), 80.

85. Babcock, "Arrange Me into Disorder", 107.

86. David L. Ungerlieder Kepler, *Fiestas Afro-Borincanas y Cambio Social en Puerto Rico: El Caso de Loíza*, (Mexico: Escuela Nacional de Antropología e Historia, M.A. Thesis, 1983), 94. This statement was made by the mayor of the village, Gabriel Santos López, in 1981.

87. Bastide, 160-161.

88. This is Ronald Grimes' "emergent" or "supine" ritual. He describes emergent ritual as having one or more of the following characteristics: it is fully cultural and historical, on the margins, a challenge to tradition, often individualistic, and sometimes self-critical. For a review of this thought, see Nathan Mitchell, "Revisiting the Roots of Ritual," *Liturgy Digest* 1 (Spring 1993): 23-26.

89. Mary Douglas, quoted in Babcock, "Arrange Me into Disorder,"
117.

5

THE TAINOS AND THE FIESTA

INTRODUCTION

Puerto Rican historian María Teresa Babín writes
that "it is not possible to dismiss [the Taíno Arawak Indian]
ethnic and cultural influence on the life of this country
[Puerto Rico]."[1]   She goes on to say that the Taíno
influence is merely concealed by the newcomers to Puerto
Rico, the Spaniards and the Africans.[2]   This chapter is
about the Taíno influence on the fiesta and its portrayal of
Santiago Apóstol.   The theoretical basis for this chapter
continues with the claims made by Gordon K. Lewis for
cultural persistence in the Caribbean and by Roger Bastide
for the possibilities of schematic similarities between
cultures that allow for the continuance of cultural forms
although in different guises.   The cultural persistence of the
Taínos recognized in such areas as language, musical
instruments, art, and the preparation of certain foods, will
be offered as examples of a Taíno remnant within the
structure and practice of the fiesta.   This remnant comes
from the Taíno religious system of worshipping gods
symbolized by *cemis*.   An exploration of this religious
system will help to bring into focus the themes located in
the annual fiesta for Santiago Apóstol in Loíza Aldea.
     When the Spaniards conquered the New World, they
often built their town plazas, with a church at one end and

the mayor's office at the other, on the same sites of the Indian *bateyes* (plazas).[3] This practice was similar to the ancient Roman Catholic practice of claiming pagan temples and turning them into churches. The same was true of the ritual performance of the fiesta in the New World. The Spaniards absorbed and reshaped the indigenous festivals they found and used them not to worship the indigenous gods but to convert the Indians to the one god of Christianity.

It was a common practice for the Spanish to indoctrinate the Indians in the New World through storytelling. Since books were scarce, and few could read anyway, religious processions were one of the best means available for telling Christian stories.[4] In some settlements in the New World the Indians readily joined these processions, "all dressed up in their best clothes, playing musical instruments, and dancing all along the route of the procession."[5] At times these processions became so popular that there was some fear that they would get out of hand.[6]

For the Taíno Arawak Indians of Puerto Rico the transition from an indigenous religion to an imposed Christianity was facilitated in part by festivals and ritual ceremonies (*areytos*) which were already in place in the Indian culture prior to the arrival of the Spaniards. Events were by and for the whole village (*yucayeque*). These festivals were held in the plaza (*batey*) and members of other villages were invited to participate. The occasion for these festivals were many: receiving strangers, celebrating victories in times of war, commemorating ancestors, rejoicing after a good harvest, the installation of a new chief (*cacique/cacica*), the marriage of a community leader, or a funeral.[7] Most likely there were processions to the plaza where soccer-like ball games (*juegos de pelota*) were played as a part of the ritual ceremonies.[8]

These festivals were important social and religious elements of the indigenous culture. Ball games, music and dancing, and eating and drinking characterized the festivities. The festivals were also the means by which the village passed on its myths, history, and traditions since the Indians had no written language.[9] In this way, the festivals of the Indians served as cultural transmitters. There can be little doubt that the religions of the conqueror and the conquered converged in part because of a shared religious form, the Spanish fiesta.

The similarity between the two festival forms is striking. The Indian festivals and the Spanish fiesta were, by tradition, ritual observances of a particular event in the communal life of the people. As well as commemorating a spirit or saint, entertainment played an important part in the festivals of both cultures. In previous chapters we discussed the Spanish and African traditions which are at the roots of the fiesta for Santiago Apóstol. It is time now to turn to the the fiesta's indigenous ground, the religion of its first people.

TAINO RELIGIOUS BELIEFS AND RITUALS

Gods

With its roots in Mesoamerica, the cosmology of the Taíno Arawak Indians revolved around male and female creator gods and their offspring. The creator gods were named *Yocahu* and *Guabancex*. Together they created the world and the cycle of the seasons. They divided the world into seven parts, air, earth, fire, and rain, with a center and an up and a down. Eugenio Fernández Méndez describes the creator gods this way:

> Accordingly, I believe that I can establish that the
> creator gods, Yocahu and Guabancex, are
> respectively: Yocahu, the old father, begetter of
> masculine power and fire, and also the son of
> Guabancex, the great universal mother. Guabancex is
> the serpent, the great life-giver and earthly mother.[10]

He outlines the Taino pantheon, the offspring of the creator
gods, this way:

MASCULINE	FEMININE
Yocahu=day=fire=air	Guabancex=water,
(Also son of the	night (Also mother
mother god Guabancex)	of the gods)
Guatauba=wind	Maquetaurie
(morning star)	Guayaba=death
	(Huracán)
	afternoon star
Boinael=sun (heart of the	Coatrisque=moon
sky)	(And heart of the
(Guanin)=son of the serpent	land)
(Boa)	God of the
	raindrops[11]

From this outline we can see that the masculine principle,
Yocahu, is the god of day, fire and air. His other names,
Guatauba and *Boinael*, show him to rule the wind, and the
sun and sky respectively. The feminine principle,
Guabancex, is the goddess of water and night, as well as
the mother of all the gods. Her other names associate her
with death and the hurricane (*Huracán*) as *Maquetaurie
Guayaba* and with the moon, the earth, and the rain through
Coatrisque. Already we can see the deep connection

between the two creator gods as well as the doubleness of
their natures.

First, each of the two creator gods participates in the
being and activity of the other. Let us begin by looking
Yocahu.

> Yocahu, the supreme divinity, son and mythic
> grandfather ... is invisible and intangible as fire, so
> omnipresent that he is called the wind, the Sun and
> the Moon. In his union with the mother god
> Guabancex he is at the same time father and mother
> of all creation. The circular form of the serpent when
> joined with fire, moreover, represents the annual
> seasonal cycle, the union of the two principal life-
> givers, the masculine and the feminine.[12]

Right away we have an interesting dynamic at work in
Taíno mythology. *Yocahu,* the invisible, the omnipresent,
is united with the feminine god, *Guabancex,* and together
they create, as fire and serpent respectively, all that is,
including the crucial seasonal cycle. Moreover, *Yocahu* is
the god of the ancestors, the old ones, those that have gone
before. He is also the father of the sun. As god of the old
ones, *Yocahu* reaches back *in illo tempore* (to the beginning
of time). As god of the sun, *Yocahu* cannot be seen, since
no one can see the sun directly. His association with
commonly held so-called masculine traits and attributes is
blurred.

> Yocahu, the father god, upholder of the world, is
> moreover especially related to the sowing of the yuca
> [cassava] as is seen in the Taíno practice of scattering
> the yuca on mountains, these same little mountains
> referring to the small plots of land of the god of the
> mountains. The name Yocahu, *Hu*--wind, spirit,

breath; and *Yoca*, the same as Yuca, reveals that the
god was at the same time the spirit of the yuca. The
root *Hu* of Huracan means wind, a mighty wind.[13]

Here we have *Yocahu's* double nature described by being
held together in a holy name. The *yuca* roots are planted
on mountains or small plots of land. The wind comes from
on high, and the yuca is planted in the earth.

As *Yocahu's* name demonstrates, the Taíno civ-
ilization was dominated by agricultural concerns. It was
also a matrilineal society in which fertility and fecundity as
the powers of the mother God were of particular concern
and, as such, they received considerable attention. The
mother god's name was *Guabancex*. She was the goddess
of the waters and the night. Eugenio Fernández Méndez
explains the connections which she has to various symbolic
representations in a brilliant word study. Her name comes
from the Taíno root *gua* which means *lugar* or place.
Fernández Méndez demonstrates that *gua* relates in so many
Taíno words to shadow (*la sombra*) and to darkness (*la
oscuridad*).

> The *guaba*, is, in Puerto Rico, the black spider and it
> is so fearsome that it is represented just as a
> blockhead or unsocial person is represented by night
> and by shadowy places.

> *Guabate*, the name of a range of mountains in the
> interior of the island of Puerto Rico, is the place
> where the clouds cast shadows.

> The *guaba* is likewise the shady tree preferred today
> in outside cafes.

> The *guabaza* is, according to Ramon Pané, the fruit

which the dead eat; Maquetaurie *Guayaba*, is, also following Pané, the Lord of the place of the dead or Coaybay.

Gabairo is in the Antilles a nocturnal bird which lives on insects, and the *Guabara* is a small crustacean which lives in the caves of the rivers.

Finally *Guacara* is a cave or temple. All of the associations of the morpheme *gua* suggest that its original meaning has something to say about the obscure, the hidden, or that which is fully dark, that is, the night. It is no wonder that the priests of the mother God or *Bohiques*, when going to visit a sick person, cover their whole faces black with the residue taken from earthen cooking pots or the charcoal taken from the pots used in milling cocoa.[14]

This study of words with the prefix *gua* is significant because these words are a part of the vocabulary of Puerto Rico today. As such, we have one example of the continuance of Taíno Arawak Indian culture in Puerto Rico's contemporary culture.

Cemis

These two creator gods, as well as their many manifestations, were symbolized by *cemis*, small triangular figures sculpted from several materials: stone, gold, human bone, conch shell, wood, and cotton. These *cemis* are more than important museum artifacts from a past era. They not only symbolized the deity, but the deity was also believed to reside within the *cemi*. Sometimes the spirits ordered that a figure be created for them as in the following story:

A tree spoke to a passerby. It told him to call the
Indian priest (bohique). When the priest arrived, he
performed the ritual of intoxication by inhaling
tobacco (la cohoba) at the foot of the tree. When the
priest fell into a trance, the tree spoke to him. The
tree told him to make a figure (cemi) for him. After
the figure was made, the priest often worshipped the
spirit in a special home (caney) constructed for the
spirit.[15]

As we can see from this story, the spirits held enormous
authority, authority which was transferred to their plastic
representations, the *cemis*. The most important *cemis* were
kept in the *caney*, the home of the *cacique*. Here they were
ceremonially fed *yuca*, potatoes, and corn. These
representations were usually of the spirits which insured the
harvest, female reproduction, and the healing properties of
the local roots and herbs.[16]

Although the social life of a Taíno village was
certainly hierarchical, two leadership roles were of equal
importance. These roles were held by the *cacique/cacica*
(chief) and the *bohique/bohica* (priest). They were the two
people who were responsible for the sacred myths and
rituals of the village. The supreme authority in the village
resided in the *cacique*. His or her major responsbilities
were to organize the *naborias*, the group which did the
agricultural work of the village, and to lead the *nitainos*, the
warriors, in the defense of the village in times of war.
Because of these grave responsibilities, the *cacique* often
sought guidance from the spirits by practicing the ritual of
intoxication (*cohoba*). When the *cacique* died, he often
became a spirit himself.

The role of the *bohique/bohica* in the village was
social, religious, and therapeutic. He taught the village,

especially the youth, about the past history of the people by telling them the great stories and myths of the village. In this way, the village insured that future generations would remember the great events of the past.[17] As a healer and priest, the *bohique's* rituals focused on the symbol of a spirit, the *cemi*. The *cemi* was crucial to the *bohique's* rituals because, as we have seen, the spirit it represented was also believed to reside within the sculpted figure. This gave *cemis* enormous power which demanded their adoration. The purposes of religious rituals employing *cemis* were twofold: to divine or prophesize and to heal. For purposes of divination, the *bohique* practiced, like the *cacique*, the ritual of *cohoba*. It began by placing a dish of burning tobacco over the head of the *cemi* to be worshipped. Then the priest inhaled the smoke into both nostrils through a "Y" shaped tube. Intoxicated, the *bohique* would then fall asleep and discern sacred messages from his dreams.[18]

Since illness and death were believed to be caused by the spirits, the *bohique's* task was to drive them away by ritual means. One account of a *bohique's* practice of healing begins with his abstaining from food. In this way he purified himself. Again using tobacco as an intoxicant, the *bohique* spoke to the spirits represented by the *cemi* in an effort to discern the cause of the illness. The *bohique* painted his face black, using charcoal from a cooking fire, as a symbolic way of taking on the sickness of the patient. After sucking on the body of the ill person, the *bohique* then spat out some small bones which he had earlier put in his mouth. This spitting symbolized the removal of the illness caused by the spirits.[19] Another story of a *bohique* exercising his healing skills describes him as massaging the entire body of his patient. He then washed the body with water mixed with roots and herbs.[20] In both reports of healing by a *bohique*, allusions are made to the powers of *Guabancex* who is symbolized by blackness, water, and herbs.   In these rituals, the *bohique* also used the ceremonial insignias of his office: his ceremonial chair (*duho*), *marácas*, and a spatula used for inducing regurgitation as a means of purifying the body before engaging the spirits.

After this brief description of the religious beliefs and practices of the Taíno Arawak Indians, it should come as no surprise that the Taínos were persecuted for their beliefs by the Church as well as enslaved by Spain for economic purposes. Chief among the targets of the Church were the *bohiques*. As custodians of the beliefs and rituals of the people, the Roman Catholic Church dubbed them *hechieros* ("witchdoctors") for their alleged "pagan" practices. And the festivals of the Taínos were replaced by the fiestas of the Spaniards.

CONTEMPORARY PARALLELS

Images of the Saint

After reviewing the religious beliefs and practices of the Taíno Arawak Indians, several suggestive associations emerge with regard to the fiesta of Santiago Apóstol as it is celebrated today in Loíza Aldea. We have noted, in the beginning of the chapter, the festival forms of the Taínos and the Spaniards were similar. Both fiestas serve social, religious, and therapeutic purposes. Each, in its own time and place, entertains and educates the people of the village. Each includes the exercise of religious obligations by the pueblo. And each, in calling upon the images of the spirit or saint, brings the people into contact with the divine.

Beginning with the fiesta proper, there are recognizable specific similarities. The dominant symbol of the fiesta, the saint, is represented by three statues. These statues are held in great reverence by the people of the village. And the image of *Santiaguito* is believed to be the most miraculous of the three. In fact, it is only around the base of his statue that tiny silver appendages can be found which symbolize the healing power of the saint. These images of the saint are small, not larger than life. Due to both their role in the fiesta and their religious importance, they can be said to represent three aspects of the saint in that there are images for the men, the women, and the children. These statues can be seen as the modern day equivalents of the Indian *cemis*. In their size, function, and use, they work in the same manner, especially with regard to the people's concerns about the harvest, children, and healing. And, except for *Santiago de los hombres*, which was made in Rome, they were constructed, as were the *cemis*, by the villagers themselves.[21]   Louise L. Cripps writes that

> As the churches stood on their old ceremonial grounds; as the crucifixes and the small effigies, the 'Santos,' replaced their *zemis*; as their old dramas and songs were replaced by Christian pagentry and hymns -- a replacement of new forms of old symbols and holy places and actions -- the transition might not have been so difficult. The forbidden old religion was artfully entwined into the commanded new.[22]

The statues of the saint are also housed in the homes of the leaders of the village. The *matenadoras*, as we have seen, wield considerable power and influence when it comes to organizing and directing the fiesta. These homes can be seen as the modern day equivalent of the Taíno *caneys*, the homes of leaders of the village which housed the *cemis*. This leads us, then, to a connection with the *matenadoras* of today and the women who served the village as the *cacicas* and *bohicas* of yesterday. Not only do these women care for the statues in their homes during the year like a *cacica*, they lead the religious observances which make up the fiesta, the prerogative and responsibility of a *bohique*. The only exception are the masses which are presided over by a Roman Catholic priest. We have here parallel structures between the Taíno festivals and the fiestas celebrated today.

Ritual Clowns

The religious beliefs and practices of the Taínos present us with another lens through which we can look at the masked figures in the fiesta. As we discussed in chapter four, the masked figures, using the generic category of ritual clown to interpret them, appear as critics of the social order. Through their disguises and antics, new possibilities for social relationships are imaginable. This is the role of the ritual clown, one who stands on the boundary, able to see both sides of the coin.

Let's look at the ritual clowns again. They naturally break into two sets of pairs. The *caballero* relates to the *vejigante*. The *viejo* is paired with the *loca*. Earlier we discussed the *caballero* and the *vejigante* in terms of the struggle between good and evil as rooted in Spain's history and Christian theology. At the same time, we described the *viejo* and the *loca* in terms of the gender relationships found within the village. We also employed trickster imagery taken from Europe and Africa to show how turning things upside down in ritual creates the opportunity to see new possibilities. Although there do not appear to be figures in Taíno mythology which are identified as tricksters, the Taíno pantheon of gods have the notion of a double nature in common with the trickster.

The creator gods, *Yocahu* and *Guanbancex*, are our model. As we saw earlier in this chapter, both gods include each other although they retain their separate identities and activities. Their representations in nature align themselves in accord with the Taíno view of a divided but overlapping world. A simple diagram will illustrate this point.

YOCAHU	GUABANCEX
up	down
sky	earth
mountains	caves
fire	water
sun/light/day	moon/darkness/night
birds	frogs
male	female
cacique	bohique
hunting	farming

The oppositions, outlined in the above diagram and which expose the double nature of the gods, appear at first glance to be more absolute than they really are. Each side of the diagram balances the other while keeping the complex relationships between the creator gods. These complex relationships are both internal and external to the gods. For instance, *Yocahu* both nurtures the harvest as sunlight and destroys it as fire. The same constructive and destructive forces are a part of *Gaubancex*. As rain, *Guabancex* nurtures the harvest. But with her coupling of rain and wind, she can be destructive. An excellent example of the internal and external double nature of the creator gods comes from recent events. As *Huracán, Guabancex's* destructive force showed itself in hurricane "Hugo" which lashed across the island in the fall of 1989. Some Puerto Ricans attribute the mitigation of its destructive power to *Yocahu's* successful battle with *Huracán*. His residence, the tropical rain forest *El Yunque,* was the mountainous place where the powerful winds of *Huracán* could not pass by. Here we have an example from nature of the conflict between the two gods while they remain doubles of each other in religious belief. These Taíno roots offer a fertile ground for the transplanting of European and African tricksters. In other words, there is no good/evil split in the Taíno creator gods, but there is a complicated configuration of interrelated positive and negative forces.

Since both pairs of our ritual clowns relate in the same way with their opposites, the *caballero* and the *viejo* can be seen as mirror images of each other which can stand in for each other. This can also be said of the *vejigante* and the *loca.* This mirroring, which we have not seen before between the ritual clowns, offers us an additional perspective on the masked figures in the fiesta as tricksters. The *caballero,* as a mask for the *viejo,* can now be paired with the *loca.* The *viejo,* as a disguise for the *caballero,* can now be the *vejigante's* partner.

In terms of all the ancestoral spirits represented in the fiesta, the Iberian, the African, and the Taíno, the *caballero* is Santiago Apóstol, *Shangó, Ogun,* and *Yocahu-Cacique,* all "sons of thunder." The *vejigante* is a trickster, *Eshu/Elegbara,* and *Guabancex-Bohique*--all images of darkness. The *viejo* duplicates the associations with the saint, and the *loca* copies the connections with the trickster.

We are seeing a pattern of relating among the ritual clowns that takes the shape of a crossroads image, that paradigmatic point at which something important occurs due to connections made, channels traveled, and doors opened, to a previously impenetratable realm. In classical mythological terms, the sky god has come down to earth, assumed its nature, making those things of the earth equal in significance to those things of the sky. The ritual clowns in the fiesta of Santiago Apóstol in Loíza Aldea allude to not only the sacredness of a particular place, the road to the beach in Medianía Alta, but they also point to the sacredness of timelessness and the ancestors. The crossroads exists on two axes: the vertical and the horizontal. The vertical axis links the ancestors and the living; the horizontal axis links the segments of the village.

OTHER TRACES

Other traces of Taíno culture can be found in Loíza Aldea today (as well as all over the island). At the roadside stands in Medianía Alta, a visitor can find *dulce*, a sweet pancake made out of *yuca*, milk, butter, spices, and sugar. Turnovers called *empanadillas* are also popular. They are a doughy mixture made from chopped crab meat, crab shell, and *yuca*, wrapped in banana leaves, and heated on a *burén*. A *burén* is a method of cooking that employs a metal or stone slab which is heated on an open fire. This practice can be traced directly to the Taínos.[23] Raymond Sokolov, writing on Puerto Rican cuisine, makes note of "the lingering Carib-Arawak-Taino traditions" for preparing Puerto Rican food.[24] Miguel Domenech, former executive director of the Puerto Rican Tourism Company, comments on the island's unique cuisine as "a savory blend of Spanish, African and Indian cookery."[25]   It is not surprising that an old Puerto Rican has been quoted as saying:

> Even today we eat the fruits and the roots our Indians
> grew. So you could say our history is living inside
> our bodies. In our bones and in our blood. That is
> why I make the saying 'If you scratch a
> Puertorriqueño, inside of him you will find a
> Borinqueño.' Our history is only skin-deep.[26]

This old Puerto Rican is marking his ethnicity by
the food he eats.[27] This continuation of the preparation
and serving of Taíno dishes shows that there were pathways
for such cultural remnants in Puerto Rico. The same is true
for certain musical instruments like the *güiro* which is still
in use by Puerto Rican musicians today. And there are
many words like *hamaca* (hammock) and place names, like
the city of Caguas, which have carved out a lasting place
for themselves in the language. In addition, at the art shop
of the late Don Castor Ayala in Loíza Aldea, we can find
art objects, crafted by the Ayala family, which portray
Taíno images. There are small *bohios*, Taíno huts carved
out of coconut, *marácas*, rattles reminiscent of the ones
used by the Indians, and busts of Taíno *caciques* or
chieftans. Don Castor Ayala has also left us a story about
how it was an Indian spirit which guided his hand when he
designed his art.[28]

With this in mind, there is ample cause to propose
that there are pathways for the survival of other non-
written, oral or ritual transmissions of culture through time.
Roger Bastide claims that when other ways are blocked to
maintaining one's cultural integrity, religion is the only way
which remains open. It is through similar institutional
embodiments that Taíno and African religion survive. It is
religion that insinuated itself into the new ways of doing
things and, in so doing, was able to continue, albeit in new
forms. To do this, the slave community adopted a posture
of acceptance, of accommodation to present realities. But

this accommodation was really a form of resistance, of perpetuating rituals even though, eventually, the gods or spirits worshipped through them might disappear.[29] Louise L. Cripps describes how this was possible in Puerto Rico:

> How some of the Indian ways were passed on is easy to conceive. It is not hard to imagine that an Indian woman, taken against her will, and hating the conquerors who had killed her husband, would take the only measures open to her for retaliation, that is through her children. They would be in her care, and it would be her pride to pass on to them such of the old ways and the old beliefs of her tribe as she could secretly do.[30]

So for Puerto Rico, not only did the Spaniards conquer and obliterate the Taínos, the Taínos infiltrated the Spanish ways of doing things because of the available structural similarities. The fiesta of Santiago Apóstol fits into the pattern. There is no physical proof, but there is the retention of a way of doing something, like cooking. Any conservation of pre-Hispanic "lifeways" is Indian according to Mary J. Weismantel.[31] This is significiant because *yuca* was more than just a subsistence crop (there were others) for the Taínos. *Yuca* was intimately bound up with its supernatural guardian and creator, the spirit *Yocahu*. It is this kind of close link between cooking and the Taíno culture that convinces me that not only cooking methods but cultural forms were also passed on through the African slaves by the Taínos, and through the African slaves to the future residents of Loíza Aldea. I have no doubt that while the culture of the Taínos is no longer prominent, thanks to Spanish domination and the influx of African slaves, a Taíno influence lingers to this day.

CONCLUSION

Since the very beginning of my efforts at untangling the meaning of the masked figures in the fiesta of Santiago Apóstol in Loíza Aldea, I have been haunted by a sense that there was a deeper connection between the masked figures than in what I was reading. I have discovered that it is in the public retelling of an ancient tale of creation, acted out on the surface as a triumph of good over evil, and below the surface as the struggle of real men and women in just simply living their lives. The masked figures meet all of their associations in the images of Santiago Apóstol when he meets the imagination of his followers.

The ground of the fiesta is in its collapsing of historical time into timelessness. This "time," the realm of the ancestors, is expressed as it only can be, in the reenactment of beginnings in a space made sacred by its appropriation for such a purpose. In the words of Victor W. Turner, a fiesta

> aspire[s] to annihilate measurable temporality, and evoke, in order to reinstate, that generative time of beginnings, to draw upon its unfailing, unstinted, and ineradicable efficacies, to redress the failures of 'present time,' to purify it of its stains, sins, and stigmata, and to restore the primeval past as paradigmatic reality.[32]

The fiesta of Santiago Apóstol returns its participants to the time "when the gods walked the earth" by directing them to walk the earth in a particular way, through a particular space. Those who walk the festival route, those who perform the age old story of beginnings by their participation in the fiesta, walk among African and Taíno images as well as the Christian saint and devil.

The ritual clowns of the fiesta, the *caballero*, the *vejigante*, the *viejo*, and the *loca*, play a role in criticizing the Iberian-Christian social order because they have lived in Loíza Aldea from its very beginnings and through all of its transformations. They are the legacy of Loíza Aldea's original people, the people of Borinquén[33], the Taíno Arawak Indians, and they are the legacy of the black slaves, the Yoruba people. These images are hidden in contemporary costumes, the masks of a dominant culture, but they are capable of being intuited by the imagination. The portrait of the *santo* is revealed in the masked figures of Loíza Aldea as they relate, in turn, to the statues of the saint.

NOTES

1. María Teresa Babín, *La Cultura de Puerto Rico*, Segunda edición (Río Piedras, Puerto Rico: Editorial Cultural, 1986), 44.

2. María Teresa Babín, *The Puerto Ricans' Spirit: Their History, Life, and Culture* (New York: Collier Books, 1971), 41.

3. Louise L. Cripps, *The Spanish Caribbean: From Columbus to Castro* (Boston, Mass.: G.K. Hall and Co., 1979), 23.

4. John McAndrew, *The Open-Air Churches of Sixteenth Century Mexico: Atrios, Posas, Open Chapels, and Other Studies* (Cambridge, Mass.: Harvard University Press, 1965), 218.

5. Robert J. Smith, *The Art of the Festival: As Exemplified by the Fiesta to the Patroness of Otuzco: La Virgen de la Puerta*. University of Kansas Publication in Anthropology #6. (Lawrence, Kansas: University of Kansas [Press], 1975), 106.

6. McAndrew, *Ibid.*

7. Labor Gomez Acevedo y Manuel Ballesteros Gaibrois, *Culturas Indigenas de Puerto Rico* (Río Piedras, Puerto Rico: Editorial Cultural, Inc., 1978), 162-164.

8. Ricardo E. Alegría does not mention processions specifically, but he does have a drawing of a *cacique* being carried on a litter by four men in *Descubrimiento, Conquista y Colonización de Puerto Rico, 1493-1599* (San Juan, Puerto Rico: Colección de Estudios Puertorriqueños, 1983), 20.

9. *Ibid.*, 22.

10. Eugenio Fernández Méndez, *Arte y Mitología de los Indios Taínos de las Antillas Mayores* (San Juan, Puerto Rico: Ediciones "CEMI," 1979), 22. The translation is mine.

11. *Ibid.* Translation mine.

12. *Ibid.*, 29. Translation mine.

13. *Ibid.*, 35. Translation mine.

14. *Ibid.*, 47. Translation mine.

15. Labor Gomez Acevedo y Manuel Ballesteros Gaibrois, 131. Translation mine.

16. *Ibid.*, 169.

17. *Ibid.*, 69.

18. *Ibid.*, 131.

19. Taken from Catalonian Friar Ramon Pané's 1505 *Account of the Customs of the Indians* as found in *The Puerto Ricans: A Documentary History*, eds. Kal Wagenheim and Olga Jimenez Wagenheim (New York: Praeger Publishers, 1973), 10-11.

20. Gomez Acevedo y Ballesteros Gaibrois, 135.

21. Alegría, *La Fiesta de Santiago Apóstol en Loíza Aldea* (San Juan, Puerto Rico: Colección de Estudios Puertorriqueños, 1954), 30, 33.

22. Cripps, 54.

23. Eugenio Fernández Méndez, *Historia Cultural de Puerto Rico, 1493-1968*, Edición Corregida (Río Piedras, Puerto Rico: Editorial Universitaria-Universidad de Puerto Rico, 1980), 49.

24. Raymond Sokolov, "In the Pan-Caribbean Kitchen," *Natural History* 97 (November 1988): 86.

25. "Inn-to Eating," *Caribbean Travel and Life* 3 (January/ February 1988): 12.

26. Stan Steiner, *The Islands: The Worlds of the Puerto Ricans* (New York: Harper and Row, 1974), 9.

27. Mary J. Weismantel, *Food, Gender, and Poverty in the Ecuadorian Andes* (Philadelphia: University of Pennsylvania Press, 1988), 9.

28. Henrietta Yurchenco, *¡Hablamos! Puerto Ricans Speak* (New York: Praeger Publishers, 1971), 43-44.

29. Roger Bastide, *The African Religions of Brazil: Toward a Sociology of the Interpenetration of Civilizations*, trans. Helen Sebba (Baltimore: The Johns Hopkins University Press, 1960), 150-160.

30. Cripps, 58.

31. Weismantel, 38.

32. Victor W. Turner, *On the Edge of the Bush: Anthropology as Experience*, ed. Edith L.B. Turner (Tucson, Arizona: The University of Arizona Press, 1985), 228.

33. Borinquén is the Taíno Arawak name for Puerto Rico.

BIBLIOGRAPHY

Acosta-Belén, Edna. "Puerto Rican Women in Culture, History, and Society." In *The Puerto Rican Woman: Perspectives in Culture, History and Society.* 2d ed., Edited by Edna Acosta-Belén, 1-29. New York: Praeger Publishers, 1986.

Alegría, Ricardo E. *Apuntes en Torno a la Mitología de los Indios Taínos de las Antillas Mayores y Sus Orígenes Suramericanos.* 2d ed., San Juan, Puerto Rico: Centro de Estudios Avanzados de Puerto Rico y el Caribe, 1986.

_____. *Descubrimiento, Conquista y Colonización de Puerto Rico, 1493-1599.* San Juan, Puerto Rico: Colección de Estudios Puertorriqueños, 1971, 1983.

_____. *La Fiesta de Santiago Apóstol en Loíza Aldea.* San Juan, Puerto Rico: Colección de Estudios Puertorriqueños, 1954.

_____. "La Fiesta de Santiago Apóstol (St. James the Apostle) in Loíza, Puerto Rico." *Journal of American Folklore* 69 (April 1956): 123-134.

_____. *Historia de Nuestros Indios (Version Elemental).* San Juan, Puerto Rico: Colección de Estudios Puertorriqueños, 1983.

Argyle, W. J. *The Fon of Dahomey: A History and Ethnography of the Old Kingdom.* Oxford: Clarendon Press, 1966.

Arrom, José Juan. *Mitología y Artes Prehispánicas de las Antillas.* Mexico: Siglo Ventiuno Editores, 1975.

Awolalu, J. Omosade. *Yoruba Beliefs and Sacrificial Rites.* London: Longman Group, Ltd., 1979.

Azúcar y Esclavitud. Edited by Andrés A. Ramos Mattei. Río Piedras, Puerto Rico: Universidad de Puerto Rico, 1982.

Babcock, Barbara A. "Arrange Me into Disorder: Fragments and Reflections on Ritual Clowns." In *Rite, Drama, Festival, Spectacle: Rehearsals Toward a Theory of Cultural Performance.* Edited by John J. MacAloon. Philadelphia: Institute for the Study of Human Issues, 1984.

Babín, María Teresa. *La Cultura de Puerto Rico.* Segunda Edición. Río Piedras, Puerto Rico: Editorial Cultural, 1973, 1986.

_____. *Panorama de la Cultura Puertorriqueña.* New York: Las Americas Publishing Co., 1958.

_____. *The Puerto Ricans' Spirit: Their History, Life, and Culture.* Translated by Barry Luby. New York: Collier, 1971.

Bakhtin, Mikhail. *Rabelais and His World.* Translated by Helene Iswolsky. Cambridge, Massachusetts: The M.I.T. Press, 1968.

Baldovin, John F., S.J. *The Urban Character of Christian Worship: The Origins, Development, and Meaning of Stational Liturgy.* Orientalia Christiana Analecta, ed. Robert F. Taft, S.J., no. 228. Roma: Pont. Institutum Studiorum Orientalium, 1987.

Baralt, Guillermo A. *Esclavos Rebeldes: Conspiraciones y Sublevaciones de Esclavos en Puerto Rico (1795-1873).* 2d ed., Río Piedras, Puerto Rico: Ediciones Huracán, Inc., 1985.

Baralt, Guillermo A., Carlos Collazo, Lydia Milagros González, Ana Lydia Vega. *El Machete de Ogun: Las Luchas de los Esclavos en Puerto Rico (Siglo*

XIX). Río Piedras, Puerto Rico: Centro de Estudios
de la Realidad Puertorriqueña, 1990.

Barrett, Laurence I., "Puerto Rico: State of Anticipation."
Time, 8 November 1993, 47-48.

Bascom, William. *Shango in the New World.* Austin:
Occasional Publication of the African and Afro-
American Research Institute, The University of
Texas, 1972.

_____. *The Yoruba of Southwestern Nigeria.* New
York: Holt, Rinehart and Winston, Inc., 1969.

Bastide, Roger. *The African Religions of Brazil: Toward a
Sociology of the Interpenetration of Civilizations.*
Translated by Helen Sebba. Baltimore: The Johns
Hopkins University Press, 1960.

Billington, Rachel. "Santiago's Golden Legend." *The New
York Times Magazine: Part 2* (1 October 1989): 24-
25,57,59,60,62-63.

Booth, Newell S., Jr. "God and the Gods in West Africa."
In *African Religions: A Symposium.* Edited by
Newell S. Booth, Jr. New York: NOK Publishers,
Ltd., 1977.

Brandes, Stanley. *Metaphors of Masculinity: Sex and Status
in Andalusian Folklore.* Philadelphia: University of
Pennsylvania Press, 1980.

Butler's Lives of the Saints. Complete Editions. Edited,
revised, and supplemented by Herbert J. Thurston,
S.J., and Donald Attwater. Vol. II: July-Sept.
London: Burns and Oates, 1981.

Carr, Raymond. *Puerto Rico: A Colonial Experiment.* New
York: Vintage Books, 1984.

Cavendish, Richard, ed. *Man, Myth & Magic: The
Illustrated Encyclopedia of Mythology, Religion and
the Unknown.* 12 vols., New York: Marshall
Cavendish, 1983.

Colón, Juan González. *Tibes: Un Centro Ceremonial Indígena*. Ponce, Puerto Rico: Editorial Kinder Printing, 1985.

Cripps, Louise L. *The Spanish Caribbean, From Columbus to Castro*. Boston, Mass: G. K. Hall and Co., 1979.

Crocker, J.C. "Ceremonial Masks." In *Celebration: Studies in Festivity and Ritual*. Edited by Victor Turner. Washington, D.C.: Smithsonian Institution Press, 1987.

Crumrine, N. Ross. "Capakoba, the Mayo Easter Ceremonial Impersonator: Explanations of Ritual Clowning." *Journal for the Scientific Study of Religion* 8 (Spring 1969): 1-22.

DaMatta, Roberto. "Carnival in Multiple Planes." In *Rite, Drama, Festival, Spectacle: Rehearsals Toward a Theory of Cultural Performance*. Edited by John J. MacAloon. Philadelphia: Institute for the Study of Human Issues, Inc., 1984.

Davies, J. G., ed. *The New Westminister Dictionary of Liturgy and Worship*. Philadelphia: The Westminster Press, 1986.

Davis, David Brion. *The Problem of Slavery in Western Culture*. Ithaca, New York: Cornell University Press, 1966.

De Oviedo y Valdés, Captain Gonzalo Fernández. *The Conquest and Settlement of the Island of Borinquen or Puerto Rico*. Translated and edited by Daymond Turner. Avon, Ct.: The Limited Editions Club, Cardavon Press, 1975.

Díaz Soler, Luis M. *Historia de la Esclavitud Negra en Puerto Rico*. Río Piedras, Puerto Rico: Editorial Universitaria-Universidad de Puerto Rico, 1953, 1981.

Dinwiddie, William. *Puerto Rico: Its Conditions and*

Possibilities. New York: Harper & Brothers, Publishers, 1899.

Douglas, Mary. *Purity and Danger: An Analysis of the Concepts of Pollution and Taboo.* London: Routledge & Kegan Paul, 1966.

Drewal, Henry John and Margaret Thompson Drewal. *Gelede: Art and Female Power Among the Yoruba.* Bloomington: Indiana University Press, 1983.

Drury, Nevill. *Dictionary of Mysticism and the Occult.* San Francisco: Harper and Row, Publishers, 1985.

Falassi, Alessandro. "Festival: Definition and Morphology." In *Time Out of Time: Essays on the Festival.* Edited by Alessandro Falassi, 1-10. Albuquerque: University of New Mexico Press, 1967.

Farmer, David Hugh. *The Oxford Dictionary of Saints.* Oxford: Clarendon Press, 1978.

Fernandez, James. "Mission of Metaphor in Expressive Culture." *Current Anthropology* 15 (1974): 119-145.

Las Fiestas de Santiago Apóstol en Loíza. Produced by Ramón H. Almodóvar and Jaime Hamilton Márquez and directed by Luis Martínez Sosa. 57 min. Producciones Vejigante, Inc. and La Fundación de las Humanidades Puertorriqueñas, 1982. Video-cassette.

The Folklore of American Holidays. Edited by Hennig Cohen and Tristram Potter Coffin. Detroit: Gale Research, Co., 1987.

Foster, George McClelland. *Culture and Conquest: America's Spanish Heritage.* Chicago: Quadrangle Books, 1960.

Fowles, George Milton. *Down in Porto Rico.* New York: Eaton & Mains, 1906.

Geertz, Clifford. "Deep Play: Notes on a Balinese Cockfight." Chap. in *The Interpretation of Culture:*

Selected Essays. New York: Basic Books, 1973.

_____. "Ethos, World View, and the Analysis of Sacred Symbols." Chap. in *The Interpretation of Cultures: Selected Essays.* New York: Basic Books, 1973.

_____. *Islam Observed: Religious Development in Morocco and Indonesia.* Chicago: University of Chicago Press, 1968.

_____. "Religion As a Cultural System." Chap. in *The Interpretation of Cultures: Selected Essays.* New York: Basic Books, 1973.

_____. "Thick Description: Toward an Interpretive Theory of Culture." Chap. in *The Interpretation of Cultures: Selected Essays.* New York: Basic Books, 1973.

_____. *Works and Lives: The Anthropologist as Author.* Stanford, California: Stanford University Press, 1988.

Gifford, D. J. "Iconographical Notes Toward a Definition of the Medieval Fool." In *The Fool and the Trickster.* Edited by Paul V. A. Williams, 18-35. Cambridge: D. S. Brewer Ltd., 1979.

Gomez Acevedo, Labor y Manuel Ballesteros Gaibrois. *Culturas Indigenas de Puerto Rico.* Río Piedras, Puerto Rico: Editorial Cultural, Inc., 1978.

Goodpasture, H. MacKennie, ed. *Cross and Sword: An Eyewitness History of Christianity in Latin America.* Maryknoll, N.Y.: Orbis Books, 1989.

Glotz, Samuel. "European Masks." *Drama Review* 26 (Winter, 1982): 14-18.

González, José Luis. *El Páis de Cuarto Pisos y Otros Ensayos.* Río Piedras, Puerto Rico: Ediciones Huracán, Inc., 1983, 1985.

Grimes, Ronald L. *Beginnings in Ritual Studies.*

Washington, D.C.: University Press of America, 1982.

Handelman, Don. "The Ritual Clown: Attributes and Affinities." *Anthropos* 76 (1981): 317-366.

Herold, Erich. *The Art of Africa: Tribal Masks.* London: Hamlyn, 1967.

Herskovits, Melville J. *Dahomey: An Ancient West African Kingdom.* vol. II. New York: J. J. Augustin Publisher, 1938.

Hieb, Louis A. "Meaning and Mismeaning: Toward an Understanding of the Ritual Clown." In *New Perspectives on the Pueblos,* Edited by Alfonso Ortiz, 163-196. Albuquerque: University of New Mexico Press, 1972.

Hoetink, Hendrik. *Caribbean Race Relations: A Study in Two Variants.* Translated by Eva M. Hooykaas. London: Oxford University Press, 1967.

Huck, Gabe, ed. *The Liturgy Documents: A Parish Resource.* Chicago: Liturgy Training Program, The Archdiocese of Chicago, 1980.

Idowu, E. Bolaji. *Olódùmarè: God in Yoruba Belief.* New York: Frederick A. Praeger, Publishers, 1965.

Ingham, John M. *Mary, Michael, and Lucifer: Folk Catholicism in Central Mexico.* Austin: University of Texas Press, 1986.

Johnson, Lemuel A. *The Devil, the Gargoyle, and the Buffoon: The Negro as Metaphor in Western Literature.* Port Washington, New York: National University Publications, Kennikat Press, 1969, 1971.

Jones, Cheslyn, Geoffrey Wainwright, and Edward Yarnold, S.J., eds., *The Study of Liturgy.* New York: Oxford University Press, 1978.

Kendrick, T. D. *St. James in Spain.* London: Methuen and

Co., Ltd., 1960.

Kirshenblatt-Gimblett, Barbara and McNamara, Brooks. "Processional Performance: An Introduction." *Drama Review* 29 (Fall 1985): 2-5.

Klein, Herbert S. *African Slavery in Latin America and the Caribbean.* New York: Oxford University Press, 1986.

Lewis, Gordon K. *Main Currents in Caribbean Thought: The Historical Evolution of Caribbean Society in its Ideological Aspects, 1492-1900.* Baltimore: The Johns Hopkins University Press, 1983.

Lommel, Andreas. *Masks: Their Meaning and Function.* Translated by Nadia Fowler. New York: McGraw-Hill Book Co., 1972.

López-Baralt, Mercedes. *El Mito Taíno: Lévi-Strauss en las Antillas.* 2d ed., Rio Piedras, Puerto Rico: Ediciones Huracán, 1985.

Lucas, J. Olumide. *The Religion of the Yorubas.* Lagos, Nigeria: C.M.S. Bookshop, 1948.

Lutes, Steven V. "The Mask and Magic of the Yaqui Paskola Clowns." In *The Power of Symbols: Masks and Masquerade in the Americas.* Edited by N. Ross Crumrine and Marjorie Halpin. Vancouver: University of British Columbia Press, 1983, 81-92.

McAndrew, John. *The Open-Air Churches of Sixteenth Century Mexico: Atrios, Posas, Open Chapels and Other Studies.* Cambridge, Mass.: Harvard University Press, 1965.

Maldonado-Denis, Manuel. *Puerto Rico: A Socio-Historic Interpretation.* Translated by Elena Vialo. New York: Random House, 1972.

Mangin, William. *The Cultural Significance of the Fiesta Complex in an Indian Hacienda in Peru.* Yale University: Ph.D. Dissertation, 1954.

Mathews, Thomas G. "African Presence in XVII Century Puerto Rican Religious Ceremonies." In *Cultural Traditions and Caribbean Identity: The Question of Patrimony.* Edited by S. Jeffrey K. Wilkerson. Gainesville, Florida: The Center for Latin American Studies, The University of Florida, 1978.

Mauss, Marcel. *The Gift: Forms and Functions of Exchange in Archaic Societies.* Translated by Ian Cunnison. New York: W. W. Norton and Co., Inc., 1967.

Méndez, Eugenio Fernández. *Arte y Mitolgía de los Indios Taínos de las Antillas Mayores.* San Juan, Puerto Rico: Ediciones "CEMI," 1979.

_____. *Historia Cultural de Puerto Rico, 1493-1968,* Edición Corregida. Río Piedras, Puerto Rico: Editorial Universitaria-Universidad de Puerto Rico, 1980.

_____. *Las Encomiendas y Esclavitud de los Indios de Puerto Rico, 1508-1550.* 5th ed., Río Piedras, Puerto Rico: Editorial Universitaria-Universidad de Puerto Rico, 1976.

Mintz, Sidney W. *Caribbean Transformations.* Chicago: Aldine Publishing Co., 1974.

_____. *Worker in the Cane: A Puerto Rican Life History.* New York: W. W. Norton & Company, 1960, 1974.

Mintz, Sidney W. and Sally Price. *Caribbean Contours.* Baltimore: The Johns Hopkins University Press, 1985.

Mitchell, Nathan. "Revisiting the Roots of Ritual," *Liturgy Digest* 1 (Spring 1993): 4-36.

Mitchell, Timothy. *Violence and Piety in Spanish Folklore.* Philadelphia: University of Pennsylvania Press, 1988.

Morales Carrión, Arturo. *Auge y Decadencia de la Trata*

Negrera en Puerto Rico (1820-1860). San Juan, Puerto Rico: Centro de Estudios Avanzados de Puerto Rico y el Caribe y Instituto de Cultura Puertorriqueña, 1978.

Morales Carrión, Arturo, María Teresa Babín, Aida R. Caro Costas, Arturo Santana, Luis González Vales, eds. *Puerto Rico: A Political and Cultural History*. New York: W. W. Norton & Co., Inc., 1983.

Moreno Fraginals, Manuel, Frank Moya Pons, and Stanley L. Engerman, eds. *Between Slavery and Free Labor: the Spanish-Speaking Caribbean in the Nineteenth Century*. Baltimore: The Johns Hopkins University Press, 1985.

Murphy, Suzanne. "Monsters, Masks & Merrymakers." *Caribbean Travel and Life*, July/August 1991, 58-63.

Napier, David. "Festival Masks: A Typology." In *Time Out of Time: Essays on the Festival*. Edited by Alessandro Falassi, 211-219. Albuquerque: University of New Mexico Press, 1967.

O'Flaherty, Wendy Doniger. *Women, Androgynes, and Other Mythical Beasts*. Chicago: University of Chicago Press, 1980.

Orsi, Robert Anthony. *The Madonna of 115th Street: Faith and Community in Italian Harlem, 1880-1950*. New Haven: Yale University Press, 1985.

Ortiz, Alfonso. "Ritual Drama and the Pueblo World View." In *New Perspectives on the Pueblos*. Edited by Alfonso Ortiz. Albuquerque: University of New Mexico Press, 1972, 135-162.

Parrinder, Geoffrey. *Religion in Africa*. New York: Praeger Publishers, 1969.

Patterson, Orlando. *Slavery and Social Death: A Comparative Study*. Cambridge, Mass.: Harvard University Press, 1982.

Pelikan, Jaroslav. *The Christian Tradition: A History of the Development of Doctrine*, Vol. 3, *The Growth of Medieval Theology (600-1300)*. Chicago: The University of Chicago Press, 1978.

Pelton, Robert D. *The Trickster in West Africa: A Study of Mythic Irony and Sacred Delight*. Berkeley: University of California Press, 1980.

Pollak-Eltz, Angelina. "Masks and Masquerade in Venezuela." In *The Power of Symbols: Masks and Masquerade in the Americas*. Edited by N. Ross Crumrine and Marjorie Halpin. Vancouver: University of British Columbia Press, 1983, 177-192.

Raboteau, Albert J. *Slave Religion: The "Invisible Institution" in the Antebellum South*. New York: Oxford University Press, 1978.

Ray, Benjamin C. *African Religions: Symbol, Ritual, and Community*. Englewood Cliffs, N.J.: Prentice-Hall, Inc., 1976.

Robinson, Kathryn. "Puerto Rico: Straddling Two Worlds." *Caribbean Travel and Life* 3 (January/February 1988): 54-65.

Safa, Helen I. "Female Employment and the Social Reproduction of the Puerto Rican Working Class." In *The Puerto Rican Woman: Perspectives in Culture, History, and Society*, 2d. ed., Edited by Edna Acosta-Belén, 88-109. New York: Praeger Publishers, 1986.

Sanday, Peggy Reeves. *Female Power and Male Dominance: On the Origins of Sexual Inequality*. Cambridge: Cambridge University Press, 1981.

Scarano, Francisco A. *Sugar and Slavery in Puerto Rico: The Plantation Economy of Ponce, 1800-1850*. Madison, Wisconsin: The University of Wisconsin

Press, 1984.

Sciorra, Joseph. "Religious Processions in Italian Williamsburg." *Drama Review* 29 (Fall 1985): 65-81.

Simpson, George Eaton. *Black Religions in the New World.* New York: Columbia University Press, 1978.

Smith, Robert J. *The Art of the Festival: As Exemplified by the Fiesta to the Patroness of Otuzco: La Virgen de la Puerta.* Univeristy of Kansas Publication in Anthropology #6. Lawrence, Kansas: University of Kansas [Press], 1975.

Steiner, Stan. *The Islands: The Worlds of the Puerto Ricans.* New York: Harper and Row, Publishers, 1974.

Sued Badillo, Jalil. *La Mujer Indígena y Su Sociedad.* 2d. ed., Río Piedras, Puerto Rico: Editorial Antillana, 1979.

Sued Badillo, Jalil and Angel López Cantos. *Puerto Rico Negro.* Río Piedras, Puerto Rico: Editorial Cultural, 1986.

Thompson, Robert Farris. *Flash of the Spirit: African and Afro-American Art and Philosophy.* New York: Random House, 1983.

Tice, D. J. "The Long Road to Heaven." *TWA Ambassador* 18 (December 1985): 29-44.

Turner, Victor W. *Dramas, Fields, and Metaphors: Symbolic Action in Human Society.* Ithaca, New York: Cornell University Press, 1974.

_____. *The Forest of Symbols: Aspects of Ndembu Ritual.* Ithaca, New York: Cornell University Press, 1967.

_____. *On the Edge of the Bush: Anthropology as Experience.* Edited by Edith L. B. Turner. Tucson: The University of Arizona Press, 1985.

_____. *The Ritual Process: Structure and Anti-Structure*. Ithaca, New York: Cornell University Press, 1969.

Turner, Victor W. and Edith L. B. Turner. *Image and Pilgrimage in Christian Culture*. New York: Columbia University Press, 1978.

Ungerlieder Kepler, David L. *Fiestas Afro-Borincanas y Cambio Social en Puerto Rico: El Caso de Loíza*. M.A. Thesis, Mexico: Escuela Nacional de Antropología e Historia, 1983.

Van Middeldyk, R. A. *The History of Puerto Rico: From the Spanish Discovery to the American Occupation*. Edited by Martin G. Brumbaugh. New York: D. Appleton and Company, 1903.

Wagenheim, Kal. *Puerto Rico: A Profile*. New York: Praeger Publishers, Inc., 1970.

Wagenheim, Kal and Olga Jimenez Wagenheim, eds. *The Puerto Ricans: A Documentary History*. New York: Praeger Publishers, 1973.

Weismantel, Mary J. *Food, Gender, and Poverty in the Ecuadorian Andes*. Philadelphia: University of Pennsylvania Press, 1988.

Welsford, Enid. *The Fool: His Social and Literary History*. New York: Farrar & Rinehart, n.d.

Willeford, William. *The Fool and His Scepter: A Study in Clowns and Jesters and Their Audience*. Evanston, Illinois: Northwestern University Press, 1969.

Williams, Eric. *From Columbus to Castro: The History of the Caribbean 1492-1969*. London: André Deutsch, Limited, 1970.

Young-Laughlin, Judi and Charles D. Laughlin. "How Masks Work, Or Masks Work How?" *Journal of Ritual Studies* 2 (Winter 1988): 59-86.

Yurchenco, Henrietta. *¡Hablamos! Puerto Ricans Speak*.

New York: Praeger Publishers, 1971.

Zaragoza, Edward C. "The Santiago Apóstol of Loíza, Puerto Rico." *Caribbean Studies* 23 (Jan.-June 1990): 125-140.

INDEX

174

ABOUT THE AUTHOR

Edward C. Zaragoza (B.A., Wheaton College; Th.M., Boston University School of Theology; Ph.D., Drew University) is Assistant Professor of Church History at Phillips Theological Seminary in Enid, Oklahoma, where he teaches courses in the theology and history of western Christianity, as well as a course in the parish ministry track of the Doctor of Ministry Program. An ordained minister in the Presbyterian Church (USA), Dr. Zaragoza has served churches in New Jersey and Ohio. He is co-editor of the forthcoming *Pulpit, Table and Song: A Festscrift in Celebration of Professor Howard Hageman* (Scarecrow).